PRAISE FOR
Tales of Horsing Around on the Trail to Success

"Horse lovers, people interested in hippotherapy, parents and care providers of children with disability will all be informed and entertained by this book. If you enjoyed the stories of James Herriot or Gerald Durrell, you would appreciate *Tales of Horsing Around on the Trail to Success*."

Mark Sciegaj, MPH, Ph.D. Professor of Health Policy and Administration, the Pennsylvania State University

"As an avid reader of both fiction and non-fiction, I am always eager to find a new and unique voice. In her stunning debut book, Edith Wislocki tells the striking and true story of incredible growth and fierce determination as she and her co-founder build a therapeutic riding center from the ground up."

Terry Stahl – chemist, avid reader

"Far from being a niche read, *Tales* is a consistently entertaining chronicle of the complexities, challenges, and joys of sharing life-changing experience with those who need it most. I was moved; Ms. Wislocki is a natural."

Randy Walters – musician, composer, consulting artist

Tales of Horsing Around
on the Trail to Success

Edith B. Wislocki

TABLE OF CONTENTS

DEDICATION *VII*

AUTHOR'S NOTE *1*

PREFACE *2*

I · EARLY YEARS *5*

II · THE MOVE *16*

III · LEARNING TO RIDE *20*

IV · HORSES AND ASSORTED OTHER ANIMALS *25*

V · LIFE AT THE NEW FARM *42*

VI · FRIENDSHIP *63*

VII · Hippotherapy *76*

VIII · Clients *84*

IX · Instructors, Therapists, and Horse Training *96*

X · Volunteers *107*

XII · The Covid Years *119*

XIII · Finances, Fundraising, and the Board *127*

XIV · Mission Accomplished *136*

XV · Epilogue *159*

Copyright © 2024 by Edith B. Wislocki

All rights reserved. This book or any portion thereof
may not be reproduced or used in any manner whatsoever
without the express written permission of the author
except for the use of brief quotations in a book review.

Printed in the United States of America

First Printing, 2024

ISBN 979-8-218-35004-8

Photographs provided by the author

Cover by Paul Weingard

Designed by Randy Walters

Dedication

This is dedicated to:

My mother and husband, who always had confidence in my abilities

Edith B. Wislocki

AUTHOR'S NOTE

This book was supposed to be titled *Tails of Horsing Around on the Trail to Success* but to an editor they would not allow the first word in the book, let alone the first word in the title, be started with what they saw as a misspelled word. I fought hard to keep the word "Tails" because the book is so much about tales of beloved animals with tails. Finally, I too had submitted to the need for accuracy of the written word.

PREFACE

On July 9, 2022, the concept of this book was born. Sheila and Bob Greenbaum, Mark and Denise Hutchinson, David Darby, and I sat on the deck having dinner. We started telling funny stories about the beginnings of Greenlock. At one point, David Darby said, "Why don't you write a book?" We thought about it a bit, told more stories, and finally, the evening came to a close. The next morning, I was driving David to the airport to fly back to San Francisco, and on my way home realized that I had been looking for something to get me through my older years. My husband had recently died and I found I had a lot of time on my hands. I was waiting to find a project that might occupy my time when it occurred to me: this just might be the project, although I am admittedly no writer.

In many ways, this project has made me become a storyteller, because I had so many improbable stories that I seemed to want and needed to tell. I decided to start writing them down in some sort of organized way by creating chapters and filling each chapter with Greenlock stories. This whole adventure of writing occurred using only my iPhone, in their app called Pages. The actual writing, only typing, took place story by story throughout the day usually sitting outside at Greenlock. And it turned out I loved every minute of it.

Some highlights about my early years: I was born on Halloween of 1944, as either an afterthought or perhaps a mistake, a hotly debated subject during my early years, for my three older siblings born a decade before me. My parents were both doctors, my mom a psychoanalyst, and my dad an anatomist and researcher at Harvard University Medical School.

My early years in school were at Milton Academy, in Milton, MA. I hated it, I was labeled as dyslexic because I couldn't read, I was a lousy student, and I experienced being bullied. I acquired my first horse, Thunder, a retired racetrack companion horse, at nine, so my life outside of school was great. Unfortunately, but perhaps luckily for me, my father died a few weeks before my eleventh birthday. Due to his death, we moved to Vassar College in Poughkeepsie, NY, where my mom became the assistant to the president at her alma mater, and I went off to boarding school, first, to North Country School, in Lake Placid, NY. It was an organically run farm school, with about sixty students in grades one through eight. The school had a barn full of animals, including fourteen horses, chickens, pigs, and dairy cows. The school had an active maple syrup sugaring off-house and extensive vegetable gardens. The students did all the farm chores and ate all the produce. Upon graduation from North Country School, I went to Woodstock Country School in Woodstock, VT. This was an ultra-progressive, non-conforming boarding school with one hundred students. The mission was to learn to value and love learning and to trust in your ability to problem-solve. Woodstock had a barn with a few horses and lots of skiing and I was always happiest when I could be outdoors. Finally, I was able to academically excel.

I loved every minute of boarding school, and I loved my mother for sending me there instead of public school. Mom was always there for me when I needed her and when I was on vacations from school, spent unconditional time with me. Most of my siblings were away at college or graduate school so I hardly ever saw them except for their occasional Christmas visits home.

After an uneventful college degree, I attended graduate school in Rehabilitation, specializing in Behavior Modification. B.F. Skinner was at his most influential during this time and I had gone to high school with his daughter. Post-degree, I started working as a behavioral psychologist with people with disabilities. With time, I got moved into managerial positions in mental health, so acquired a second graduate degree in Human Service Administration.

During this time, in 1979, I married my husband, Al Darby aka Sweetie. I had moved into his Rehoboth house a year earlier. We finally built a small barn so I could get back into riding, and we had two golden retrievers. As time went on, I realized I really loved what I was doing but hated going to work.

My midlife crisis started to take a form. I started trying to figure out how I could combine my degrees and professional interests into being outdoors on a farm with my horses and dogs. The plan of Greenlock finally jelled. My husband, Al was incredibly supportive; my siblings were indifferent. My mom had died two years before Greenlock was dreamed up and established, but she would have completely loved and supported my new venture. And my one motherly regret is she never knew about it.

Greenlock Therapeutic Riding Center's mission is "to provide therapeutic recreational riding to people with disabilities." This book is about the improbable stories that happened behind the creation of this mission.

CHAPTER I

EARLY YEARS

Greenlock Therapeutic Riding Center was started and incorporated in 1989. The name Greenlock comes from a combination of the names Sheila Greenbaum and me, Edith Wislocki, the founders of Greenlock. Both of us were having a midlife refocus on our careers: I had a real job in mental health administration where I had to dress up and look professional, but really, I wanted the rest of my life to include my golden retrievers, horses, and jeans; Sheila had taught special education and had three grown children who were leaving home, so now she, too, was looking for new opportunities. We both had recently acquired horses, lived close to each other, and so became trail riding buddies. During these rides, when we weren't being bucked off, I described my fantasy of creating a therapeutic riding center in Rehoboth, Massachusetts, to Sheila.

Although Sheila and I thought we were reasonably accomplished riders, we decided to take lessons once a week at a local farm five miles from our homes. We rode our horses to Palmer River Riding Club and after an hour lesson, rode home. Palmer River Riding Club was an actual club that had been set up in the '50s as a place where people from the Providence, RI area who bought stock in the club, could keep their horses and ride. The facility covered about forty acres and was a gorgeous piece of property, but the farm itself was extremely run down. The board of directors who ran the facility had very little money to put into its maintenance, so they leased the farm out to people who could manage a horse facility. At the time, the managers, Kim Morgan and her husband were leasing the farm and teaching riding, mainly dressage and eventing.

As I spent more time at the farm taking lessons from Kim, I got to know more about the facility. After a couple of years, Kim revealed that they were leaving to start a similar facility on the West Coast. Perhaps it was my destiny to rent this farm to see if I really could start a non-profit therapeutic riding center.

Leasing the farm proved to be the first of many adventures. The board was less than inviting to my initial inquiries, mainly because I wanted to focus on people with disabilities. They did not want the farm to give up its focus on being a boarding stable that also taught riding and was a riding club. I asked Paul Antonellis, my then boss and friend, to assist in writing a rental proposal to present to the board that would be acceptable to them. Two facts were obvious: the buildings were falling down, and the amount of rent money being asked was especially high.

There was a barely livable house on the property which had, in the distant past, been divided into two apartments. This turned out to be crucial in the lease proposal. Maybe we could lower the proposed rent cost by half by repairing infrastructure at the market value each month to make up the rent difference. That turned out to be acceptable to the board and a three-year lease was signed. Additional lease obligations included our continuing to board horses and giving lessons to the local community. If we could find a barn manager/instructor to live in one apartment and a contractor to live in the second apartment, we could possibly make a go of it. By this point, Kim, whose lease was not yet up, discovered what was being proposed, and in no uncertain terms told Sheila and me that we lacked enough horse savvy to undertake such a business!

There's nothing like a thrown gauntlet to motivate. I immediately turned my attention to becoming incorporated and gaining a non-profit 501c3 status. I found a pro bono lawyer who navigated those challenges. Incorporating was easy, but the non-profit status took time and included setting up a board of directors, appointing officers, and creating bylaws. It took almost three years to receive our non-profit status. During this time, I made numerous calls, which were always answered by Charles Gillette, our IRS coordinator, to sort out what still had to be done to prove that a farm with horses really qualified for non-profit status. We finally received our 501c3 approval letter in August of 1991. The letter was typed on a Selectric typewriter, (for those who don't remember Selectric typewriters, they were forerunners of word processing in that they could remember a form letter so the typist only had to change keywords before sending out the particular form letter) and it was addressed to Greenlock Therapeutic Riding Center. However, the third paragraph said, "After review of the revenues derived from the operation of the Royal Caribbean Classic Golf Tournament, we have concluded you are exempt from federal income tax." A Selectric mistake. Emotionally, I was simultaneously laughing and crying, hysterically. The next morning, I called Charles yet again. I read him the letter. Silence, an expletive, followed by an order to immediately tear up the letter, with an assurance that a corrected letter would immediately be sent out. A corrected letter finally arrived; the original letter is still intact.

Now that I had a farm, and the pieces of creating Greenlock started falling into place, I realized that this was a big undertaking to do alone. On one of our infamous trail rides, I asked Sheila if she wanted to become part of this adventure as partners, with us each putting in $10,000 as starter money to be paid back before we became salaried. Her answer was yes, and she replied, "I thought you would never ask." That was the start of what became a great friendship and the creation of a successful organization that has brought many laughs and so much joy to so many people.

So, in July of 1989, we had a three-year lease agreement at Palmer River, with a takeover date of September first. We needed a person to take care of the eight horses that would remain boarding with us, and the five horses we needed to find to start our program, all of which needed to be trained. We needed a contractor to do the required monthly renovations, we needed licensed riding instructors for both disabled and regular riders, and we needed therapists. The one thing we didn't need was clients. The word was out and people wanted to come to Greenlock. Before we even leased the farm, at least thirty people were on a waiting list for services.

Solving the staffing gap actually turned out to be easy. My neighbor, Joe, a teacher, who in the summer renovated houses and built barns and gazebos, was getting a divorce and needed a place to live. A free apartment in return for carpentry work was a perfect solution, and he had his own tools. A riding instructor, Joan Davis, whom we both knew very well, was about to get married and needed an apartment, and a rent-free apartment that included her taking care of the horses and teaching abled body riding lessons, was another perfect solution. After she moved in, we did not see her husband Tom for at least a month. When he finally did emerge, it turned out he was a horse trainer and riding instructor who had grown up on a horse farm in Vermont where his mother, Heather St. Claire Davis, a well-known horse show judge and equine artist, bred event horses.

Liz Baker, a physical therapist, who was a colleague of mine, wanted to come work with us and set up the hippotherapy program. She brought with her a student, Sue Fiske, who was finishing her degree as a physical therapy assistant (PTA). Sue is still working with us to this day.

We found Lisa Powers, who was a Massachusetts-licensed riding instructor. She also was one of the first therapeutic riding instructors licensed by a grassroots organization that later became known as North American Riding for The Handicapped (more about that later). Lisa was to become our first employee. She was an extrovert, who was beautifully young and energetic, had manicured nails, always wore ironed white shirts, and embraced our weaknesses and saw them as sort of funny. She was a hit, and everyone loved her. It was beginning to seem like Greenlock had some sort of magic that attracted wonderful people to help out and get involved.

We started with five horses. Copper, an older Quarter Horse, was perfect. He came to us as donation. Todd, a huge Quarter Horse Thoroughbred, was donated by a friend. Sweet William was another large, black, older horse that we were told was "serviceably sound," a horse euphemism for "… he's lame but you can still use him." Budweiser, given to us by a friend, was an older pony who looked just like a Clydesdale. He had been there and done it all. And we had Trixie, a pony rescue owned by Lisa Powers, our new riding instructor.

We stayed at Palmer River for three years. During this time, Lisa taught all our therapeutic riding lessons with the assistance of Sheila and me, and Liz Baker ran all the hippotherapy sessions. The number of riders was always on the rise and we had numerous contracts with schools and agencies to send us students. The original agency was the Genesis Fund, which was under the auspices of National Birth Defects in Boston. They funded about ten riders who wanted to start as soon as we opened our doors. Additionally, the Justice Resource Institute sent a group of troubled teens, and Liz Baker brought about eight community-based clients she wanted to start in the hippotherapy program. Soon after, we got a contact with St. Mary's School in Providence. This was a residential school for young girls who, for many reasons, no longer lived at home and had various learning issues. From that point, word of mouth spread the news of our program, as did various newspaper articles.

Lisa taught one of our most memorable riders, John (Jack) Hawkes, an emeritus English professor at Brown University. He was a postmodern novelist born in Connecticut, educated at Harvard University, and was an author of numerous books. He was happily married to Sophie, whom we never met. Lisa became his second love. He would only take lessons from Lisa and preferred to have his lessons on Sweet William. Jack was a fixture at Greenlock. He said his disability was his age, therefore he figured he qualified for our services. Jack gave us all signed copies of many of his books, and as we were readers, there were many provocative literary discussions. Jack was also hard at work writing another novel which, when published in 1991 was titled, *Sweet William*.

At this time Sheila had an elderly goat, Rufus, who lived at her house, and somehow the topic of the goat's eventual demise came up when Jack was about. Jack asked if he could come and watch the goat being put down when the time came. When the day arrived in 1990, Sheila invited Lisa, Jack, and me over for the event. She served us lunch and then the vet came. Rufus was loaded into a trailer and then the vet gently injected Rufus with drugs which put him to sleep. Jack was thrilled with the experience and thanked us all profusely. A year later, after his book *Sweet William* was published, the reasons for the goat event became evident: it was all part of the novel. In many ways, the entire novel was about his time with us at Palmer River.

One of the first needs that became apparent almost immediately, was that a farm needed a tractor and that Sheila and I needed to be the operators. Luckily, we had an elderly farmer friend, Arthur DeMattos, who drove an old red dump truck with a hood ornament that was a rearing horse. He always called us "the girls" or "you girls." He had an old tractor for "you girls" that he practically gave us, and he taught us how to drive it. Arthur came to the farm one or two times a week to mentor the "girls" farming progress. Our tractor training was uneventful except when the first time Sheila did a solo drive, she backed into an old fifty-gallon drum of used motor oil. It had been left behind by our predecessors and it sprung a leak. Oil was rapidly dripping out of the tank towards the manure pile, and I knew oil was not environmentally friendly. Luckily, the hole was near the top of the drum, so I could scoop oil out into buckets to avert a total environmental disaster. I called Arthur, who came, yet again, to our rescue. He took the drum away so "the girls" wouldn't hit it again. Arthur and his red dump truck saved us many times in our first few years, including taking all the farm's manure away and bringing us endless truckloads of clay to make horse stalls functional. One day years later, he appeared with a rearing horse hood ornament as a gift to me, because he realized I loved it. Today it resides as a piece of art in my house.

The lease at Palmer River required us to board horses. A boarder is someone who owns a horse and needs a farm where it can live and be cared for. This seemed like a great idea since it provided a monthly guaranteed income of $500 per horse and there were eight boarders, so that was $4,000 per month. That was the upside. The downside was that the boarders often had very different requirements for the care their horses deserved and/or required.

Let's start with stall care. Each horse, on average, produces forty pounds of manure and about two gallons of urine per day. Accordingly, if a horse is out of its stall for eight hours per day, that leaves a lot of urine and manure in its ten-by-ten-foot stall in a twenty-four-hour day. Our job was to clean this up on a daily basis to the satisfaction of each boarder. Boarders are happiest if they arrive at the barn to find their horse's stall filled with clean shavings and no manure. Greenlock's policy was to do a deep clean on stalls weekly, add clean shavings at that time, and pick stalls daily to clean up manure and wet spots. Herein is the problem: most horses do not stand still in their stalls. Therefore, the manure is mashed into the shavings, producing dirtier and dirtier shavings as the week progresses. Slowly, the boarders got unhappy. They either complained or after we had left for the day, raided the shaving pile and added more shavings. Additionally, many boarders felt that if there is even the possibility of snow or rain, they do not want their horses out. One boarder was so insistent on this point that if she happened to come to the farm in inclement weather and her horse was out, she went and brought him in. This strategy had one flaw: she couldn't catch her horse unless she caught all the other horses first and returned them to their stalls. Then she would catch her horse and put all the other horses back out. We loved watching this!

Our dear boarders also had feeding requirements for their particular horses. Our school horses all ate the same food without supplements and remained healthy and active. Boarders' horses all had different food requirements, and most had multiple supplements added to enhance their diet. Some had as many as three different grains, mixed with two-three supplements, twice a day. All horses had hay two or three times a day, but hay was a hot commodity for boarders, and many gave extra hay as a treat, especially after they rode. Thin horses were never a problem. In fact, on at least two occasions when outside trainers came to give riding clinics for boarders, it was pointed out that their horses were "ample," i.e., overweight.

Boarders' horses also had wardrobes of blankets for every season and every temperature. These consisted of blankets in at least two weights for cold nights. In addition, they had sheets to keep them clean, coolers to cool them out after work, fly sheets to keep flies away, and raincoats so they could go out on a rainy day. And, yes, we put them on and took them off, based on specific criteria set by each boarder. Our horses, of course, were without wardrobes. Because horses naturally grow their own winter coats, who through evolution have evolved, our herd looked shaggy all winter and wet when it rained, but then again, they are just horses.

An additional problem was rats. Palmer River was a tired, old farm and the rats had turned it into condo living! Sheila and I were not really aware of how severe the problem was because we went home by six, but the boarders came at night after work, and they were well aware of the problem. Thus, the complaints started. Being ecologically minded, we started solving the problem with dogs and cats, but it turned out we had the only dogs (three golden retrievers, one border collie, and one Jack Russell terrier) and cats who seemed to like rats! We moved to the next level: locked rat bait boxes. That lasted about two weeks because our barn manager was now doing target practice by throwing pitchforks at them and occasionally impaling one. It was not the fastest or most appealing way of solving the problem, hence we finally called the local pest control to rid us of rats. This they did for the next two weeks. Dead rats were everywhere. The word was out: no more condo living at Palmer River.

Joe, our builder/repairman, did amazing things to try to upgrade the buildings. He fixed the new barn and hay loft doors, installed new windows, sided buildings, repaired the hay loft to prevent collapse under the weight of hay, and performed endless repairs to the house. Joe seemed relatively happy living at Palmer River. His sons stayed with him on weekends and he spent summers in his cottage on the Cape, but Joe was having a lot of emotional difficulties due to his impending divorce. Over the second winter with us, this became most apparent. One night I got the first of many memorable calls: Joe's truck was parked in the far reaches of the property and he was unconscious. The ambulance was called. He ended up in the hospital and got the care he needed. He remained at the farm with us until we moved and never had another episode.

A men's group in town who called themselves "The Cosmic Cavemen," had a mission to become self-actualized (very trendy in the '90s), and they volunteered to do infrastructure repairs. They came twice with at least ten men and did two major projects. The first was to paint the entire barn, and the second project was to re-roof and re-shingle a six-stall barn. All labor and repair costs done by our contractor and volunteer groups went towards our rent. We never missed our infrastructure agreement payments nor on our monthly agreed-to rent.

An ongoing challenge during our three years at Palmer River was raising enough money to cover our expenses. This included paying back the $20,000 Sheila and I put up-front to get us started. Because this process of achieving 501c3 status took over two years and was not finalized until 1991, we could not ask for tax-exempt donations. Our only alternative for these additional monies came from capitalizing on the local horse community, who were always looking for horse shows and opportunities to take lessons from well-known riding clinicians. We put on three or four benefit horse shows each year and had another two or three riding clinicians doing two or three-day workshops. Palmer River had an indoor riding arena, two outdoor riding arenas, and fifteen acres of fields and wooded areas with jumps, a great site for these activities. During our stay there, many people paid to truck their horses just to use the space the farm had to offer, and, of course, they also wanted to participate in all our events. An added benefit was that the schooling shows could include some of our therapeutic riding students, along with riders from the community at large. So, we paid the clinic and show costs and charged the riders to participate. The difference belonged to us.

One of the more exciting events that happened spontaneously while we were at Palmer River was Bozo the Clown. One of our friends who took lessons at this farm had a grown daughter who was the producer of the Bozo television show (aired from 1982-1994) and she asked if Bozo could spend an afternoon at Greenlock. What a hit! Bozo came in full regalia and watched some of our riders. We then invited all of our riders and friends to come and visit with Bozo. Unbeknownst to us, some of our boarders dressed their horses and themselves up as if in a parade. Baggins was ridden by Minnie Mouse (Pat), and led by Mickey Mouse (Bob). Janet dressed her huge, gray, Quarter Horse up as Jumbo – trunk and all – and Sheila brought her daughter's pony, Apple, who pulled a cart that could seat eight kids. Bozo rode around the farm many times that day in the cart, followed by Baggins with Mickey and Minnie Mouse, and Jumbo. They were surrounded in turns by many of the kids who rode at Greenlock with us. About one hundred people showed up for what became known as a Weekday Afternoon Extravaganza. Apparently, we were on the next edition of The Bozo Show!

We loved our three years at Palmer River, but it was time to move on to our new farm, and a new chapter in the Greenlock story. Dawn Cook took over the Palmer River lease, and finally, she was able to buy out the stockholders. She now owns Palmer River and has turned it into a world-class riding center. To this day she remains one of our good friends and supporters.

Bozo Extravaganza

CHAPTER II

THE MOVE

Greenlock stayed at Palmer River for three years and we were now a viable business with a non-profit status. We wanted to move to our own farm with none of the baggage of renting a run-down farm with boarders.

The house my husband and I owned in Rehoboth that had belonged to Peter Amaral. The Amarals sold their house to us and moved next door, down a long driveway where they had a small eleven-acre farm. Years before Greenlock was even a fantasy, we had obtained a first option to buy this property if they ever moved. Once again, destiny was on our side. Ten months before our lease ended, they were moving and asked if we still wanted to buy. Yes, and now I had a small farm to move Greenlock to. Incidental to this purchase was the fact that Sheila lived around the corner from me and could also ride or walk to the farm.

After they asked if we wanted to buy the farm, I suggested to Sheila that we trail-ride our horses over from Palmer River to show Lisa the property that I was going to purchase. We rode the five miles through mostly woods and approached the property from the back where there was a brook that had to be crossed. We had crossed this stream many times, but I decided to approach the crossing a little further upstream.

My horse's front legs went into the mud up to his elbows, but his hind legs stayed on the embankment. Mr. Tye lunged three times to try to get out. I then decided to dismount, but, simultaneously, he lunged a fourth time. I toppled forwards and sideways. My front teeth bashed into the saddle horn before I landed, unfortunately, on a sapling that had been cut and was sticking two inches above the ground.

Blood was coming out of my mouth, my front teeth were resting against my palate, and it was painful to breathe. I thought I might be having a heart attack. Sheila handed me her bandanna and said, "Don't look, just don't look." To get home I had to get back on the horse and ride the quarter mile back to my house and leave the horses in my barn. Sheila took me to the Sturdy Memorial Hospital's Emergency Room, and Lisa rode back to Palmer River. Luckily, I was not having a heart attack. Instead I had two broken ribs and was then sent to a local dentistry surgeon who put my top teeth back in place and cast them for a month, after which I would undergo root canals. Lisa's farm visit was short but memorable.

We moved to our Summer Street location in the summer of 1992. Before we moved, we had to build an eight-stall addition to the small barn, fence in all our paddocks, and build a riding arena so we could function year around and in inclement weather. Lisa, our riding instructor, was leaving to get married. She had mentored us enough that we had our MA state riding license and our therapeutic riders license so we could now teach. Our barn managers, Tom and Joan, were also moving to their new farm on Joan's mother's property in Rehoboth. So, we had to find a new barn manager who would live in the three-bedroom house on the property.

Again, Greenlock might have gotten lucky! There was a couple, Bob and Pat Rock, who lived in Rehoboth and boarded their big black Percheron gelding, Bilbo Baggins, at Palmer River. They wanted to move into the Greenlock house so they could live with, and take care of, their horse, and bring their overly indulged, often neglected, standard black poodle, Gus, with them. They sold their house and moved into the Greenlock house to become our first barn managers. Bob was an engineer and Pat was an artist, who kept reminding us that she belonged to the Providence Art Club, which she thought made her among the artist elite.

Bob wanted to build the stalls, especially the stall for Baggins, so he enlisted my husband Al, who knew nothing about carpentry, to help him. Every Saturday for three months they built the eight stalls needed.

Sheila's brother, Bruce Nelson, dug all the fence posts, one hundred and six, and then, with Sheila's and my help, put up the three-rail fencing. Neighbors who wanted firewood cut trees to make pastures, and my stepson, David moved rocks for stone walls. To this day he blames me for his back problems.

The biggest and most expensive project was to build a sixty-by-one-hundred-sixty riding arena. This structure was to be built about three hundred yards away from any other structure on the property. For this, we needed a loan, and loans are pricey, so I decided to lend Greenlock the money with no interest. At the time we built this arena, contractors were begging for work, so we got a quote for $80,000 along with a building permit, and four months later had an arena. All we needed now was an occupancy certificate from the town. Promptly, the fun began: the town Plumbing Inspector said we needed handicapped bathrooms for both males and females since we had new construction and it had to be in compliance with 248 CMR sec 2.10(19)(L) of the state law. Up until now, we had been using handicapped porta johns, but they no longer qualified. In order to build two bathrooms at the arena site, we would need a new septic system, a well, and heat for the bathrooms. None of this made much sense or was financially possible. I talked to many people and finally discovered that I could appeal to The Board of State Examiners of Plumbers and Gas Fitters in Boston. So, I decided we should argue to build one unisex handicapped bathroom attached to the house, which is between the barn where we tacked up, and the riding arena where we rode the horses. Arguing for building only one bathroom required we substantiate that many bathroom users had opposite sex caretakers assisting with toileting. I went to Boston and met with a group of about sixteen men, all plumbers and gas fitters, who kept referring to me as "the little lady." After much talk, they approved the plan. Once this plan was approved, although the bathroom had yet to be built, we got our building permit from the town. We never gave up the porta john and is still used at Greenlock today.

Finally, moving day came and we trucked our horses over to the new Greenlock location. The Rocks had moved into the house a few days earlier. The first night the horses were there, we had a very small Champagne barn celebration to inaugurate the farm. Two months later, some friends of mine, the Sanders, came down from northern New Hampshire and threw an outdoor turkey roast at our new arena so Greenlock's staff, volunteers, participants, and neighbors could see what we were up to. The party was a success! About eighty people showed up and we consumed eight turkeys.

Aerial view of Greenlock

CHAPTER III

LEARNING TO RIDE

There are a lot of terms in riding that have meaning for real riders but mean nothing to people who only think they know how to ride. Some examples: half halts, engagement, bending, flexion, elasticity, not to mention leg yields, half passes, and collection. Horses need to be supple and have their hind ends engaged to provide much of this, whatever that all meant. Actually, a good analysis of what it all meant was horses need to be like ballet dancers: flexible yet strong, and their riders had to have the ability to ride them in a way to optimize this happening. Unfortunately, Kim was right. We knew very little, and we were starting down the long road of learning. Luckily, Lisa embraced our deficiencies, found them amusing, and started our education. We had learned to ride by pulling back on the reins to stop the horse, to go left you pulled the left rein, right, the right rein, to go forward you kicked the horse, so speed and direction could be easily regulated. This version of riding was slowly but surely going to change.

We embarked on every possible assistance we could get when we leased Palmer River. We had lessons from countless local instructors: Tom, Joan, and Tori, to mention a few. We had people come and do various clinics, such as Linda Tellington Jones, a well-known New

England instructor, and we had a world-class rider, Eric Horgan from Ireland, do four-day workshops twice a year. He made his livelihood by doing clinics across this country for three months at a time, and then he went back to Ireland for three months on his farm. Luckily, most of the cost of this was covered by boarders who always want important people to watch and teach them to ride. In retrospect, Eric Horgan must have wondered about us. He had us hooked! He was handsome and had a voice to die for; female riders clung to his every word. I remember one day early on, when he was trying to teach me the concept of bending, how to get a horse to bend to the left and to the right when going in a circle. He was holding a dressage whip, which is about a yard long, and he was bending it left and right and comparing it to how the horse's rib cage should look. I was still clueless.

During these early lessons at Palmer River, we were riding our own personal horses. Sheila had a mare called Tammy, a black Morgan Quarter Horse cross, and I rode a Quarter Horse gelding named Mr. Tye. We both dearly loved our horses and thought them to be perfect in every way; somehow, we overlooked the fact that Tammy regularly ran away with Sheila, so she started buying stronger and stronger bits, euphemistically called the "killer bits," to make Tammy stop. I, on the other hand, was regularly being thrown off due to Mr. Tye's shying at shadows, so I resorted to western saddles so that I could hold onto the pommel.

Our instructors were less than happy about our horse choices, especially Sheila's horse, Tammy. To an instructor, they said she was physically very stiff and psychologically set in her ways. They suggested she sell Tammy and find a new horse more suited to her newly acquired riding skills. Sheila finally decided that Tammy should get sold, and she found a buyer who wanted to use her as a breeding mare. Sheila thought that would be a great life for her so she agreed to the sale over the phone. Sheila then asked me to help her trailer Tammy to her new home forty miles away. We arrived at the farm and it looked pretty new with a huge barn/indoor riding arena. The stalls were in the middle of the arena and riders rode around the stalls, a bit odd, but that was their way. We left Tammy in her new stall and went to the log cabin house with the buyer to get a check and work out the sale. Sheila was in front of me as we went in, and she suddenly turned to me and said in a very serious voice, "Don't talk, don't say a word!" And in we walked to a house filled with exotic stuffed animals, end tables mounted on elephant legs, stuffed heads mounted on every wall, gazelle, giraffes, warthogs, hippopotami, lions, tigers, and a grizzly bear standing up on its hind legs. Skins were on every floor and on all the leather couches and chairs. I was silent; actually, I was speechless. When we left and I could finally talk again, I said, "Wow! You sold her to a big game hunter! I think Tammy's head will fit right in on one of those walls."

Mr. Tye remained my lesson horse. He had the physical ability to do what our instructors wanted although, unfortunately, I did not have the skill set to ride him properly. Additionally, I thought I really wanted to learn to jump real jumps on a horse. Mr. Tye quelled all these ambitions because to be successful at jumping, the rider needs to be confident. I was not. So, in turn, Mr. Tye found jumping scary. He often cantered up to the jump, abruptly stopped, and said, "I don't think we should do this!" I went sailing over his head onto the ground, sometimes on the other side of the jump. In spite of all these challenges, he actually remained with me and became a school horse at Palmer River during our tenure there. Later, Tom and Joan took him to their new barn as a school horse when we moved to our new farm.

Over the early years of my learning to ride, there were memorable moments when breakthroughs happened. One day I was riding a horse we had acquired named Arthur, a big Appaloosa, and he had a somewhat hard mouth, meaning he ignored a rider pulling back on the reins to stop him; and all of a sudden, I understood "elastic hands." The object was not to stop him by pulling power because he's a strong horse. Instead, it was to have "elastic hands" and guide his movement by keeping a light contact with his mouth through the reins. From there, the "half halts," a subtle way of saying, "Listen! Pay attention!" started to make sense. From that day on, I rode with "elastic hands." However, in the scheme of things, it was only a small, but necessary step forward.

Sheila and Edith learning to ride at Palmer River

Another major breakthrough in my learning to ride occurred only after moving to our new location when I was taking lessons from Bruce, a retired higher-level dressage rider, who became our instructor at the new farm. I was riding my horse, Taylor, and I asked Bruce to get on Taylor to warm him up at a walk for five minutes, and then I got on. Wow, what had he done? Taylor was a different horse! I could feel the power of his back. He had a different sensitivity and a willingness to move with such lightness because he was engaging his hind end and I could feel what it was.

From Bruce and Taylor, I also learned how to bend a horse. I learned what flexion was, and I learned to sit back in the saddle rather than leaning forward, which was the root cause of my being bucked off on all our early trail rides. Leaning forward had always felt safer to me, but exactly the opposite was true. All of these concepts I had heard instructors tell me over and over again, but I realized I was a person who had to learn by feeling, not from words, and once I felt it, it was mine.

Sheila was also learning these critical riding skills but she learned all this much more quickly than I. Then again, she took many more vacations than I did, and she retired at least twice, so I had much more time in the saddle to finally become a better rider. Her mastery of these skills resulted in her entering some novice events, which are horse shows in which you have to demonstrate competency in dressage, cross-country jumping, and stadium jumping. Competition and jumping scared me so I never felt the desire to compete on horseback.

CHAPTER IV

HORSES AND ASSORTED OTHER ANIMALS

The horse is at the heart of our program; no horse, no program, and every horse had to be the right horse in so many ways, but above all a safe and happy horse.

Over the years, horses came and went, some being more memorable than others. The right horses remained with us for years, most living well into their late twenties, many being with us for fifteen to twenty years. The major factors for their longevity with us: they had to embrace what we do, be safe in doing it, and show that they liked doing it. Ordinarily, there were about eight or nine horses at our farm.

Finding the right horses is one of our most difficult tasks. We reject at least nineteen out of twenty horses offered or looked at. This task of finding the right horse fell to Sheila and me with assistance from others. Usually, if we took a horse, they came on a trial for thirty days. When we first started, most of our horses were donated. As the years went by, donations became rarer, horses became more expensive, and people selling horses were more reluctant to let there be a trial.

The initial step to see if a horse would work for us is often unforgettable. The whole process generally starts with a phone call, when we try to ferret out any issues that might suggest the horse will not work for us. My experience suggests that every horse has a weakness and owners usually are upfront about it in a very veiled way. An example might be they say the horse is somewhat fit, and the translation might be, it runs away with you; or they say a horse is alert on a trail, which often means it suddenly spooks at things; or the horse had an injury last year but will be fine for what you do, translation the horse is lame. If we get through the phone interview to our satisfaction, we set up a visit to see the horse. These visits are always an adventure. Often, we go and the horse is obviously not a settled horse, or the horse is very nice but needs a more active job than we can offer, or the horse is lame. Other visits are more remarkable.

Years ago, a call came in about a ten-year-old Standard Bred, who had been a harness racer and was not performing well but had a sweet, settled disposition. Were we interested in a donation? Sheila and I had heard great things about this breed so we agreed to go look. We got to the barn and met the horse, who had extremely long legs and did have a sweet demeanor. Because it was a harness racing barn, they had no saddle, and no ring - just a race track, so I volunteered to jump on him bareback and go for a ride. I asked him to walk – nothing. Sheila led him to get him started and I tried again. He stopped. I tried to turn left – nothing, right – nothing. Finally, the stable hand turned to us and said in broken English, "No one ever on him before." I remained calm and pretended this was an everyday event, as I sat on this horse who had never felt a rider on his back. I realized that day that harness racers don't need to be ridden, and I had not asked the obvious question, "Has he ever been ridden?" We said "no" to taking him back to Greenlock because he would have been a big project.

On the upside, many years ago, I saw a sign on the side of the road saying, "Horse for Sale." I stopped, and in the barn, tied in a straight stall was one of the most perfect horses I had ever seen. His name was Odin and he was a Haflinger, seven years old, green broke, which means he could be saddled and bridled, and someone had been on his back and survived. They had no ring, just a grassy path between two stone walls. I got on him and rode up and down, without incident, so I said I'd take him. At this time, I was still young and energetic. This seemed like a fun project. I went home, hitched up my trailer, got a check for three thousand dollars, and went back to get Odin, but he would not, come hell or high water, get on the trailer. The owner reassured us saying, "Don't worry. We will deliver him tonight," and they did. Odin stayed with us until he died at age twenty-nine. He was one of our beloved stars and the start of our quest for the breed. Today we have four Haflingers working at Greenlock.

Another adventure occurred when we went to look at a horse at the Franklin Park Zoo in Jamaica Plain where the Boston Mounted Police stabled their horses. One of our vets now worked at the zoo and thought one of their horses might be perfect for our program.

Sheila and I decided we trusted this vet's opinion so once again we dragged Sheila's horse trailer behind our truck to go access the horse. Getting to Franklin Park Zoo involved going through Mattapan. At that time Mattapan was one of Boston's least inviting suburbs, and we just wanted to get through the five-mile stretch of the inner city driving.

All was fine and we finally got to the Zoo, got out of the truck, and discovered that the trailer ramp which, when up and locked, served as the trailer's back door, had vibrated open and fallen, so we had been dragging it through Mattapan, with sparks flying from metal being dragged on asphalt. The metal on the door where it had been dragged was sheared off. The amazing thing is no one in Mattapan even seemed to notice. We had stopped for at least fifteen lights, and it had been a slow trip through all the traffic, but our passing went unnoticed. The horse was not one we could use, but the staff was very helpful in securing the door for our return trip.

One of our other successful visits was to see a pony without a name, just called Pony. Sheila and I brought Kathy, a volunteer at the time, whom I called my indentured servant because she was around so much for this visit. We arrived at an extremely fancy estate in East Greenwich where two horses resided. One was a reasonable-looking horse, but the other was the pony, later to be named Freckles, a sad, underweight pony, who had the biggest swayback I have ever witnessed. Swayback means a horse's back has dropped so their back looks like a bowl, and in his case, it was a deep, deep bowl. Other than his obvious swayback, he seemed great. We left without making a decision, and went to McDonald's for lunch. Incidentally, this luncheon choice became a horse visit/lunch destination from that day on: Big Mac for me, Fish Sandwich for Sheila, and fries. It was clear at lunch that Sheila and Kathy were smitten and were going to save this "free to a good home," pony. I was skeptical but said okay. After our gourmet lunch, we went back, loaded Freckles, and took him back to Greenlock. They were right! He was a hit and everybody loved him. We started using him immediately. Even our picky therapists, who only wanted a horse with perfect conformation, loved using him. In spite of his swayback, he remained with us for another seventeen years. Occasionally, when we had important visitors, I tried to hide him, for I never really got over his swayback.

Sheila and I went up to New Hampshire to look at a Haflinger mare called Annie. She looked great and was the perfect size. She lived in someone's backyard. Once again there was not a great place to ride her, but we were undaunted, so each of us got on her briefly. In retrospect, the family seemed uneasy with our rides, but we attributed this to the fact that they had no horse experience. This was their daughter's horse, and she had left for school. We took the horse as a donation and returned to Greenlock. Now the fun began! Horses have great memories, and sometimes an early event in their life traumatizes them forever. The event remains a mystery to future owners, but when events trigger this memory, the horses react without a thought. It's a fight-or-flight response. Annie did not like things suddenly happening behind her. If something behind her startled her, she bolted forward. We were never told this and now it was clear why her previous owners were concerned with our casual rides. We tried many ways to cure Annie of this affliction. Everyone liked this horse, but we finally gave up, and she went to another barn in Rehoboth where they taught higher-level riding. To this day, she remains at this barn and she still bolts when startled, but they love her.

Sheila and Laurel Welch, one of our physical therapists, found us a white Arab called Gemini, which we changed to Jiminy. Arabs are known to be a hot breed, translated as very energetic, but also highly intelligent and intuitive about what is happening on their backs. We have had at least four Arabs since we started. The other most notable one was Toby. Arabs need calm and experienced riders in order to ride them, but they seem to understand if they are being led, that the child on their back is fragile, and needs to be handled with care. One day Sheila suggested that a teenage volunteer, Rosalie, who loved Jiminy, and whose family was friends of Sheila's, get on Jiminy for a ride. She started riding in our ring, and all was well, so they progressed to a small path, called the track, that circumvented our indoor and outdoor arenas. I was sitting in the arena office looking out the window when all of a sudden, a white flash galloped by with Rosalie on top. I heard Sheila screaming, "Ho, ho, ho!" repeatedly at the top of her lungs. The next thing I knew, the flash passed the window again. I got up, went out, and Jiminy was still racing out of control around the track. My thoughts were: this is not going to end well. He passed the window a third time, racing out of control, and I screamed, "Steer him into the outdoor arena!" Rosalie started to, then lost her balance and hit the ground. I thought she was dead. Sheila ran to her, but she got up, said she was fine, and thanked us for letting her try Jiminy. She never asked to ride him again. From that day on only a few people were allowed to ride this horse, but in his sixteen years with us, he never lost one of the Greenlock clients. He was a great horse, who had spoken, saying, "I'll do anything for your clients, but I'm not interested in being ridden," and we heard him.

We took a horse named Redd, a Morgan, who was with us for about four years. Morgans are known for growing tails long, thick, and full. We acquired Redd in October and his tail was completely wrapped and enclosed in a canvas bag about eighteen inches in depth. We were told not to touch or remove the bag, and that his donor would come back in late April before the horse flies reappeared to "harvest his tail!" She returned as promised with large scissors, tail conditioner, a clean towel, and huge elastics She unwrapped the tail, which was full and thick, and now fell to the ground and extended out almost two feet. She added conditioner and brushed the tail until it glistened. Then she cut the tail in a straight bob about six inches below the tailbone, bound the harvested hair with elastics, and wrapped it in the towel. These four feet of hair would be sold at a good price to various of buyers, who would make hair extenders for less fortunate breeds who grow paltry manes and tails, or to people who make horse-hair jewelry, or for fly sticks that riders carry on trails to help keep bugs off their horses. The horse had been donated to us but she made good money on harvested tail!

Recently, we went to look at a Welsh Cross pony that an employee of ours had found advertised on Facebook for what seemed like the right price. We got to the barn and were looking at this extraordinarily beautiful, perfect-sized, and well-proportioned pony who was being tacked up for our visit. I sensed there was something wrong, for there was no way this was a $5,000 pony! So, I asked, "Incidentally, how much is the pony?" When they said "$50,000," I started laughing. We explained the mix-up, which had come from Facebook posting rules around selling and pricing. But, I wish we had that pony.

More recently, we found two seventeen-year-old Haflingers for sale with a requirement they go to the same home. I called and the first question I asked was, "Are they herd-bound?" A herd-bound horse cannot leave the presence of the other horses without a temper tantrum. "No, they were not herd-bound," was the answer. At seventeen years of age, this made sense if they had been handled properly. We went and looked, liked what we saw, and made an offer contingent upon a one-week trial. We brought them to our farm and the next day we planned to work with them one at a time. Let the rodeo begin! We got Rocky out of his paddock, started up to our arena, and we had an out-of-control, unfocused, whinnying pony on our hands. His friend, Rosey, was no better. She was galloping around the paddock whinnying at the top of her lungs. We got to the arena, shut all the doors, and tried to give Rocky some gentle, yet focused, work, to no avail. He was beyond listening to any humans. After twenty-five minutes, we switched and worked with Rosey and had the same result. I checked in with the owner and described our concerns. She said yes, this had been a problem in the past and it might take them a month to settle down. What happened to the answer to my original question that they were not herd-bound?

Lest we forget, Rosebud was a Draft Quarter Horse mare donated to us by Tish Bodell. Tish later became a volunteer, as did both her teenage sons. Rosebud came with a companion miniature donkey called Amigo. Amigo is still with us today, although Rosebud has passed on to greener pastures.

Much to everyone's annoyance, I referred to Amigo as the "World's Most Useless Donkey," since he earned no keep, except occasionally being asked to make an appearance at a Providence bar for Cinco De Mayo. It turned out I was very wrong about Amigo. One day about four years ago, a lawyer from Providence came to the farm with her sister, Libby, who had been diagnosed with Alzheimer's. They asked if Libby might come and visit Amigo two or three times a week and spend time brushing, walking, or just sitting with him while he grazed. Libby came, with a companion, to be with Amigo for three years until she had declined enough and could no longer make the trip. Amigo clearly knew when she drove down the driveway because he would immediately come to the gate and bray at her in a greeting. It became an amazing relationship over the three years. Amigo had become a therapy donkey. About three months after Libby's last visit, her sister called and told us Libby was in hospice at her home in

Cranston, RI, and her final wish was that we bring Amigo to see her one last time.

Our visit was set up for a Sunday morning. We loaded Amigo onto a horse trailer and headed for Cranston. We got there, unloaded Amigo, and walked into her small front yard. The whole neighborhood had turned out, including the rescue squad, who had lifted Libby, in a chair, down to her front yard. There was no question in any of our minds. Amigo recognized Libby and Libby recognized Amigo. Amigo rested his head on her lap, and Libby placed her hands on his head. They spent about twenty minutes together. It was poignant and heart-wrenching, but so uplifting that it had worked out so well. Unfortunately, Libby passed away five days after our visit. Two weeks later, Libby's sister once again arrived at the farm and presented us each with a bound book of all of her black and white drawings. It turns out she had been an artist, who, for the past thirty years, had done political and social justice cartooning for many major newspapers. For the three years she had come to the farm, none of us knew this. Amigo had earned a place in our therapeutic riding program. He needs no therapists or riding instructors to make his magic happen, and another woman who also developed Alzheimer's is now visiting with Amigo.

Soon after Libby's passing, one of our volunteers, Karen, developed cancer. When she was strong enough, she returned to the farm, just to be with Amigo. She would walk, talk, and cry with him, and he seemed to understand. They would sit together for hours, and she took strength from their relationship. When her cancer was gone, she returned to volunteering, but she still visits Amigo two days a week. He became her therapist.

Horses are social animals. All our horses live in paddocks with sheds to go into at night, and by day they are part of a herd. We believe that horses need to be horses if they are going to be happy, and living in social herds is natural for them. Generally, in any herd, there is a hierarchy and the herd then divides into smaller groups of two or three horses who graze together, eat hay together, or just hang out with one another. This all works until it is time to bring a new horse into the herd.

This usually starts with a horse trailer pulling down the driveway. All our horses line up at the paddock fence to see what we have brought to their farm. Lots of whinnying and posturing ensues from our herd while the new horse is unloaded and whisked off to his own paddock and stall so he can play the look-and-see game for a day or two. Then the introductions begin in earnest. We start with putting the new guy in a paddock with the horse at the bottom of the hierarchy. Usually, this goes smoothly, so then we introduce the next guy in the hierarchy into the paddock, and so on until we get to the top horse. It's the rare horse for which this plan works without incident. Typically, somewhere early in this process, the herd decides that they don't like the new guy so they start chasing him, ostracizing him, perhaps kicking and biting him. At this point the new horse is taken back to his private space; we rethink our strategy and try again the next day. This process can take a week or a month. We have introduced many horses into our herd over the years, and we have only had one horse injured and one horse that could not gain the herd's acceptance.

The horse we could not integrate was a Paso Fino gelding, named Mosa. We really liked this horse because the breed is bred for the way they walk, trot, and canter. All those gaits are exceptionally smooth and noticeably different from how other horses move. We liked Mosa's movement because we could teach riders who were not well-balanced safely. But, not one other horse at Greenlock liked Mosa. At any opportunity they got, they chased him away, tried to bite him, kick him and sent him to the far end of the field to eat by himself. He never made an equine friend in all the years that he remained here. This was a therapeutic riding center; we are sensitive people, but our horses were anything but sensitive. Bring in a horse that was a little different and our horses said no.

The horse that got injured was called George, and he was a great big, dark bay Thoroughbred. Normally, we did not take great big horses or Thoroughbreds, but we were persuaded to try George. He'd been with us about a week, and back then Sheila and I cleaned paddocks, so Sheila suggested we put him out with the other horses since we were there cleaning paddocks and could supervise. I suggested this might not be the best plan, but Sheila persisted so I agreed as long as she remained vigilant in monitoring this plan. Ten minutes passed and all was going well. Sheila had gone to another area to clean paddocks. I was filling water tubs and I looked over at George to see blood squirting out of his head, and shooting up about six inches in the air. I screamed for Sheila to look at George. When she finally did, she ran over to get him out of the paddock, screaming, "Call the vet, call the vet!" I got cloths so she could put compression on the wound. Blood was everywhere! I called our vet, Corrina, who calmly got on the line, telling me it would be an hour before she could come and not to worry because horses' heads bleed a lot, and anyway, horses have lots of blood. Meanwhile, clients were about to arrive. I told Sheila she had to move George out of the parking lot because this was not appropriate for our families to witness. After an hour of compressing, the vet arrived, and, yes, the wound did not even need stitches. However, an artery had been hit causing a massive amount of squirting blood. This happened in mid-August, the height of fly season. Of course, when I checked on George the next day, his wound had maggots crawling around. I once more called Corrina. She came, cleaned them up, and told me, in no uncertain terms, that the maggots were only trying to assist in wound management. George did not stay with us past his trial period because of his size. He was a sweet horse. However, try as I might, therapists just will not use big horses, even great horses who are big because they feel it is not safe to have their riders up so high when most therapists are short.

 We have always had wonderful veterinarians, beginning with Bristol County Veterinary Hospital started by Amy Hurd, DVM, who became one of my dear friends and a person truly committed to the mission of Greenlock. One of her colleagues was Corrina

Barry, DVM, who to this day also remains a friend. Amy ran a mixed animal practice so she treated our horses, my golden retrievers, who were omnipresent at the farm, and our one barn cat, Ellery. Amy was loosely associated and hung out with Mike (Mikie) Schobel, who was a kind of town mayor, and whom everyone knew. He always had a cigar in his mouth, loved his beer, and hung out at the local racetracks. He also dealt with dead or dying horses. His skill with horses was amazing, if not a bit unorthodox. Mikie was known to jump on any horse presented to him, even if he knew nothing about it. He had draft horses who competed in horse pulling events at all the local fairs. Amy, on the other hand, was a practicing Christian who never entered any place that even sold alcohol. An unlikely pair indeed, but nevertheless, a devoted pair. Both he and Amy became our friends, and unfortunately, both developed Alzheimer's, Mikie, first. Amy took care of him until he died. Soon thereafter, Amy was diagnosed and went downhill very quickly. Such a sadness.

Annual care for horses from a vet includes about four to six vaccines. Additionally, they get dewormed twice a year by us, and a dentist comes to file their teeth down annually. Horses' teeth grow longer throughout their life, and since they no longer live off the land, eating and having to grind coarse vegetation with their teeth, a person must come and float (file) their teeth with a huge file that can be bought at any hardware store. Oddly, most horses seem to enjoy this dental experience. Most horses need to wear shoes, due to the fact that some previous owners thought shoes were a good idea. The downside of this decision is that the horses' soles become weakened and sensitive, so they must continue to wear shoes or they become foot sore. A farrier comes every eight weeks to shoe our horses. Our farrier, Bob Vierra, has been with us since we started Greenlock and he is still with us today. Bob is truly one of the funnier people I know and he is a master storyteller. Every time he comes, my staff crowds around him to hear his latest exploits. I have never seen him have trouble shoeing any horse.

When Bruce, our trainer, had his fancy dressage horses boarding with us at the new farm, he had his own farrier come to shoe them. It took hours and Bruce came to help because his horses were constantly trying to bite and kick the farrier. One day, I suggested Bob shoe his horses, and Bruce agreed. The horses stood quietly for the entire process.

Other health care for horses comes in the form of treating a horse who is sick or injured. The most common affliction horses get is colic. Colic is the number one killer of horses and since our herd is usually on the older side, we have seen a lot of colic in thirty years. Usually, colic presents with a horse not eating or a horse constantly trying to lie down and roll and showing signs of discomfort. My analysis suggests that colic presents itself in one of three ways: gas colic, impaction colic, or twisted intestine colic. Gas colic, the mildest of the three, can usually be cured by us giving the horse Banamine, an anti-inflammatory, to control its discomfort until the gas passes. If this does not work, then we move to the next level of impaction colic. This requires a vet to come, rule out a twisted intestine and then pass a tube from their nose into their stomach and siphon in a gallon of mineral oil mixed with water and electrolytes. Hopefully, in twenty hours, you get oily manure, and *voilà*, the impaction is free! Twisted intestine is by far the most serious and results in the horse's death unless very costly surgery is performed. Over the years, we have lost three older horses to this form of colic.

We briefly had a middle-aged horse called Handyman, who came from Rehoboth, and he was a great addition to our program. Unfortunately, on Christmas night he colicked, so our vet Corrina came out and got him through the night. But over the next three or four days he was not right and was slowly going downhill. Corrina came daily and was baffled by his lack of progression. It finally became clear that he was not going to make it, so we had to make the heavy decision to put him to sleep. Putting a horse to sleep is easiest if you can do it in a trailer of some kind, so the body can be taken to an appropriate site that will dispose of its remains. Handyman then was put on Mikie Schobel's flatbed trailer and covered with a blue tarp. Corrina was not happy with herself and wanted to know what she might have missed in her treatment. She asked if she could do an autopsy on Handyman. We said yes. The autopsy occurred the next morning, Sunday, when no one was about. Mikie came, and Corrina appeared in tall rubber boots up to her knees with the largest carving knife that I had ever seen in her hand. Apparently, that was all she needed to check out the stomach and intestines for the cause of the death. An hour later she was satisfied with the cause: gastritis which is inflammation of the stomach wall. The remains were covered with the ubiquitous blue tarp, and Mikie drove the horse to his final resting place. The golden retrievers at the farm were fascinated by the whole process and considered the autopsy site theirs to smell and keep well marked for weeks to come.

When we acquired Jiminy, he came with a letter of instructions that said he did not need to wear a blanket in wintertime, since he would grow a good winter coat. This was music to my ears since most horses are better off without winter blankets and they are a nuisance to put on and off. For two years, he colicked about three times a year, and one day I noticed that he was holding himself sort of rigidly and I thought, perhaps he was colicking because he was cold. I gave him a winter wardrobe and his colicking stopped. Another lesson learned is not listening to what previous owners said about their horses.

The most serious disease our herd has ever gotten was a disease called strangles. Strangles is like a severe cold with coughing, snotty noses, and very swollen glands in the horse throat area with pockets of pus, hence the name strangles. Unfortunately, it is highly contagious and often fatal.

When I was about eight years old, I hung out at Mr. Peterson's barn up the street. He was a farmer who used draft horses to work his fields and had a Hinny, a cross between a stallion and a donkey, and one other riding horse. I loved to hang out with his horses.

One late afternoon I happened to be at the barn when he put his horse on crossties and then took out his jack-knife and thrust the little blade into a huge pus pocket under the horse's chin. At least a cup of white pus drained out on the floor. I remember it all so clearly, and the horse survived. When we had strangles at our barn I told the vets this childhood story, but they said in this day and age antibiotics are the treatment of choice. Since losing two horses to this disease, one of whom had these huge pus pockets, I wondered if the old way might have worked, but I didn't have to courage or confidence to try it.

The disease came to Greenlock because one of our riding instructors asked if she could take Rosebud, one of our horses, to a trail ride event called a Hunter Pace. We agreed, they went, had a great time, and three days later the horse got sick. Two days later all but two of our horses came down with symptoms. Amy and Corrina were here morning and night trying to assist us with managing this outbreak. Our barn was quarantined, and staff had to wash their shoes off in bleach before leaving the farm. This went on for about three weeks, and we lost two horses to the disease. Needless to say, we never let another of our horses leave our property to go to the functions that included other unknown horses.

We acquired a pony named Spot, who was our first Pinto pony. He was quite old, but the perfect size, so for weeks we tried to make him a happy Greenlock horse. But he was a little strong in the mouth and a little too forward and energetic, so we decided to sell him to a good home only. A family came to look at him and had some concerns about his age. Their daughter had recently lost her pony and they didn't want her to lose another one. They asked me about his longevity and I said he seemed fine but was of an unknown age. They decided he was too strong for their daughter and left, a lucky move on their part. That was on a Friday. On Monday, I arrived at the barn and Spot was stumbling and staggering around, bumping into trees, rocks, and the fencing. I called the vet. Amy came right out and diagnosed a neurological condition with seizures. Spot did not recover and was put to sleep that morning. Once again Mikie came with his two-horse trailer and a draft horse to get the body. He attached a long rope to Spot's halter. The rope went around a pulley in the trailer and back to the draft horse's pulling harness. The draft horse pulled Spot's body into his trailer. Mikie then loaded his draft horse, which climbed right over and around Spot's body in the same trailer and departed Greenlock.

Our belief at Greenlock is that if a horse has worked with us, we will take care of it until its life is over. This means we have all the sadness that the end of life brings. It also brings huge remains that have to be appropriately disposed of. One of the more concerning issues is that if the horse has been put to sleep in a humane way, it is now filled with powerful drugs that stay powerful for a very long time. So burial, which in many places is not legal, but is done because it is cheap and convenient, means these drugs could leach into the soil and water supply. Over the years we have respected this environmental issue and have resorted to other means of disposal, such as composting or rendering. It's a complex problem.

We also spent time just having fun with our herd of horses. Yearly we rode in the annual Rehoboth Memorial Day parade. In winter, after snow storms, we would saddle up and pull people on sleds behind the horses. On the Saturday before Christmas, we rode the horses around singing Christmas carols to our neighbors. Many weekends a group of us would go on trail rides over the Rehoboth countryside. One time when we were off riding, we ran into an eccentric neighbor riding their camels through the woods. Our horses did not like this encounter at all; to a horse, they wanted to head for home. It's said that horses never forget. On future trail rides when we got to this spot, the horses always looked for the camels.

Most trail rides were uneventful, but on one such ride, seven of us went, Bob Rock on Baggins and six women on other assorted horses. Bob was concerned that the pace was too slow. He said he and Baggins were going to leave us so he could ride at a faster pace. Off he went at a canter. We continued on and four minutes later, Baggins was back, without Bob. We grabbed Baggins' reins and found Bob sheepishly walking back to the group. He was fine, but his bubble had been burst.

Sometimes our trail adventures included putting horses on trailers and taking them to faraway places. The most fun was going for a beach ride, most often in the winter season. The horses seemed to like all our downtime adventures. It gave them a change in routine and it was always fun for us.

Dogs have always been very much a part of life on the farm. I have always had two golden retrievers following me around, and Sheila had a golden that I gave her from my brief attempt at breeding dogs. From the perspective of our monitoring agencies, dogs are not allowed. Greenlock has always violated this rule because our town has a no leash law, and neighborhood dogs hung out at the farm all the time. They loved all the people and constant activity. Additionally, we had wild deer, coyotes, and turkeys, not to mention loose cows, llamas, and the fore-mentioned errant camels, who lived a few houses away and had taken rides about the neighborhood. Our horses have to expect the unexpected, and I believe it is best to have a herd of horses that accept other animals, including dogs, as just part of their everyday life.

Our neighbor acquired guinea hens, which were loose most of the time, and of course, they gravitated to Greenlock at least twice a week. Guinea hens make an amazing amount of noise and they totally disrupted our ability to have riders on horses. If we tried to chase them away, they started to squawk and run in the opposite direction of where we wanted them to go. Our dogs thought they provided great sport and the birds seemed to have little ability to run from this danger, beyond zigzagging, as a flock, in various directions. One day they were directly behind our arena, and so we called their owner, Tanya, who appeared elegantly dressed in a wool skirt, silk top, shawl, wool dress hat, and farmer's rubber boots. She was carrying a long staff and started chasing the hens towards home. The hens had no interest in going home so they ran, squawking, followed by Tanya, in any direction except the one that led home. Tanya remained in pursuit to no avail. Tanya's family's adventure with the guinea hens was short-lived. They could not persuade this breed of fowl to go into their coop at night, so the local coyotes finally feasted on them.

Another neighbor, Heather, had chickens and one beautiful and friendly rooster. Often, Heather walked over to visit Greenlock in the afternoon. On this particular afternoon, she had not realized she was being followed by her rooster. When she appeared at the arena door, the dogs got up to greet her and saw the rooster fifteen feet behind her. That was the demise of the rooster. The dogs were now playing tug-of-war with it, and the humans were trying to disentangle the dogs before the riders saw the mayhem.

As I have mentioned, cows constantly visited Greenlock, but the strangest set of usual nightly visitors were two feral cows who cohabited with a now feral pig. We could not figure out why our lawns were being turned over in patches of dirt overnight until the threesome was finally seen. The pig was rooting for grubs every night. Nobody admitted to knowing who the animals belonged to. The animal control officer spent weeks trying to catch the trio, and as time passed, they became more brazen about visiting during the daylight. Finally, they were chased into a confinement area and caught.

Lastly, wild Canadian Geese are always about. Tabouli, one of my golden retrievers hated geese and chased them from our pond whenever they were about. We liked the service she provided. One day in late March, when Tabouli was getting on in years, a goose was swimming in the pond after we finished Saturday sessions and Tabouli went after it. We finally realized the goose couldn't fly because it kept frantically swimming from one end of the pond to the other with Tabouli in pursuit. No amount of cajoling would get Tabouli to stop her quest. Given her age, I was sure Tabouli would expire and drown. But Emily, one of my fabulous therapists, handed Kris, one of our volunteers, her wallet, hat and phone and jumped in the frigid dirty pond fully clothed to catch Tabouli and give the goose time to escape to a safer location. Now, that's employee loyalty!

CHAPTER V

LIFE AT THE NEW FARM

Greenlock's history at the new farm could be divided into different eras based on who our barn/farm managers were. The job of a barn manager has dramatically shifted over the past thirty years. When we first moved to our new location, we only had eleven acres, mostly woods and pastures, so horse and barn care, along with minimal lawn maintenance, became the focus of our barn manager. As we acquired more land and equipment, the job shifted to farm maintenance and less about horse care, with the exception of morning and night horse feeding, which remained the one constant task of all farm and barn managers. The reality of it was that Sheila and I mostly enjoyed and were capable of doing horse care. Although we thought we were up to the task of farm maintenance, we quickly realized we really lacked the skills, and strength, and motivation to maintain a growing farm.

THE ROCK YEARS (1992-1998)

Pat and Bob Rock were our first barn managers and they stayed for about five years. The Rocks were wonderfully concerned with the horses, but they always had requirements that went far beyond the necessary: we had to set boundaries for them. One of their requirements was they had to bring their own trainer, Bruce Graham, who later it turned out, became so instrumental in teaching me to ride and was, a huge asset to Greenlock for many years. The downside was that Bruce brought with him two high-level dressage horses to board at Greenlock. There went the "no more boarders" rule. These horses lived in their stall twenty-four/seven, except when being ridden by Bruce. That meant shavings, lots of shavings, and we said no, if you want shavings you buy them. Our horses no longer used shavings since they all had stalls with access to paddocks. Of course, if Bruce used shavings for his horse, Baggins also had to have shavings and so began the have-and-have-not horse years. The have-horses also had a wardrobe of blankets, fans for the summer heat, and nightly late-night snacks. The have-not horses were our school horses, who were much loved by everyone, but mostly lived in social herd without shavings, blankets, and fans. Since horses are herd animals, this is a more natural life for them.

Pat Rock loved living at Greenlock, but she had very unpredictable moods. It was never clear what kind of Pat would come out of the house in the morning. Her husband, Bob, announced that all the work at Greenlock was Pat's responsibility since he had a full-time job as an engineer, but he was willing to help with building projects. We needed a tractor and tool shed, and Bob was willing to embark on this project, once again, with the help of my husband. We felt this was such a small project that there was no reason to acquire a building permit from the town. How wrong we were! The shed was a very simple design, all built on the ground, starting with pressure-treated boards, and four-by-four uprights that were to enclose a tractor shelter with an attached small walk-in tool shed. The roof was peaked and covered with rolled roofing, and the sides were covered in rough-cut boards. The greatest part was the shed was potentially movable. It was all simple and cheap until the building inspector showed up and put a cease-and-desist order on the structure.

The first infraction was that the shed needed an inspected foundation, which met code and dug into the ground in six places. It was not especially easy when the structure was all built, and secondly, the roof infrastructure needed to be able to withstand the weight of twelve inches of snow. Thus, it became known as the Polish shed since our builder built the shed before he built the foundation (my husband named it that because of my last name). Since the Polish shed was movable, we dug six two-foot holes six inches from the movable shed and poured footing two feet deep with pressure-treated four-by-fours placed in the concrete. Then we moved the shed onto the footings and used hurricane fixtures to attach the shed to the footings. It was easy enough conceptually, but it took weeks. The roof infrastructure was no problem to fix since we had an engineer on our side. Finally, we had a building permit that didn't even require handicapped bathrooms!

Soon after the Rocks arrived at Greenlock, they decided they needed a second horse, Nicky, in order for them to have his and hers horses and ride together. Nicky soon became the most entitled horse at Greenlock, along with Baggins. Nicky was decked out in black leather tack with all brass trim and purple pads and blankets which matched Pat's clothing perfectly. Baggins had black tack and silver trim. Baggins was a black draft horse who had a white star in the center of his head. Bob would get upset in the summer when his black coat developed a dark brown tint from the sun, so Bob decided to feed him a supplement that was supposed to turn his coat black again. Unbeknownst to him, I was applying some ash to his white star which made it look gray, and one day I said that the supplement is definitely working. Even his star is starting to turn black. Bob looked at the graying star and stopped the supplement.

Pat took two days off a week: Sunday and Wednesday. The other days she fed, cleaned stalls with my help and taught a handful of riders. In the summer, she mowed the one-acre lawn around her house and mowed the two acres of pasture twice a year.

The Rocks brought Bruce Graham to Greenlock. Bruce lived in Rehoboth with his partner, Russell, who later became his spouse, and he brought his two horses, Sweeter and Aran, to Greenlock. Both horses were warmbloods, which really means they were bred to become performance horses in the upper reaches of equine sport. Bruce had been an accomplished dressage rider all his life and was known for buying, training, and selling rogue warmbloods. A rogue horse is a horse that becomes intractable and untrainable, usually because humans have badly mishandled the horse at an early age so they no longer trust people. Other horses are deemed rogue because they are energetic and have an independent spirit, which, if handled correctly, can be channeled into amazing partnerships. But, foremost, the horse must trust its trainer. Sweeter, a mare, who loved Bruce, was an older and very talented, dressage horse that Bruce had trained and kept as his other partner. Aran was a younger, also talented, rogue horse that Bruce was training to sell. Bruce remained part of Greenlock for the next twenty-five years giving us lessons and helping us out with training new horses that came into our program.

The Rocks considered Bruce to be their mentor and he gave them both dressage lessons with Bob on his Percheron, Baggins, and Pat on her newly acquired Quarter Horse, Nicky. Pat took extra special care of Bruce's horses. One morning, I received a phone call from Bob, who was in the emergency room with Pat. He told me that a horse had bitten off the tip of Pat's finger and I needed to go up the barn and get the glove which was in the trash with finger in it. My first response was, "Oh no! Which of our horses had done this?" And then I wondered what would the glove look like, and when would the lawyers call, all the stuff of nightmares. I got the glove, which had a hole where the left index finger would have been, but there was only a spot of blood. I called Bob back. Apparently, the fingertip was no longer necessary to the finger repair, so I was instructed to return the glove to the trash. Pat arrived home about noon time and it turned out that Aran was the culprit. He had been nibbling Pat's hand, which was resting on his stall door. He took one final, big, nibble that resulted in the fingertip being compromised. It was now stitched and bandaged. Thank God it was one of Bruce's horses because they could do no wrong!

One of the problems that existed at the farm, haunting us for the next twenty years, was loose cows. Two of our neighbors owned cows and they were constantly getting loose and coming to our greener pastures. The owners seemed unconcerned because cows usually went home at the end of the day, and the town's response to the problem was: there are no leash laws for dogs and apparently that applies also to loose cows, pigs and goats. We kept trying to herd them into the road so they would become a town nuisance, but they were reluctant to leave our grassy areas. Pat had created beautiful flower gardens of which she was very proud, around the Greenlock house. One day, two cows were standing and eating in her gardens and she tried to shoo them off. They ignored her and continued eating. She then took after them with a long whip. They ran around the house with Pat in pursuit. The cows reappeared at the front of the house and Pat reappeared, too, whip and all. They jumped her picket fence, ran through her garden, and ran back behind the house again. She jumped the picket fence and continued after them. Finally, on the fourth trip around the house, which always included jumping the picket fence, with Pat still in pursuit, also always jumping the picket fence, they decided to go to the barn and then into the woods. It was pretty funny and I was laughing so hard that I was no help. The problem with stray cows coming to Greenlock persisted for years, so we learned to accommodate their occasional presence.

During our third year at the new farm, we had a major problem with birds, particularly English sparrows, living in our new riding arena. There were well over fifty nests with birds pooping, birds squawking, and baby birds falling out of nests all over the arena. We tried many ways to solve this problem, including hanging a fishing line in doorways, as is done on ship spars. The wind moves ships so this works for ships, but not for us. We tried putting fake owls in the arena, but fake is fake, even to sparrows. We also tried building screen doors, but the birds waited until we had to open doors to go in and out, or went under the doors. These birds always found ways in and out. At this time in our history, we would close Greenlock for a week every July, so I quietly decided that during this week we would seal up the arena to get rid of the birds. Most of us were away and the Rocks were instructed not to enter or let anyone enter the arena. The week passed and the day came to enter the arena again and there was silence. I expected to find dead birds but only found two, and remarkably, no birds have, to this day, ever nested again in the arena, with the exception of one family of robins. This happened, in spite of having reroofed the arena, and erected sheds attached to the arena where we tack up horses, and where birds are allowed to nest. I suspect many baby birds died in their nests that week, which became imprinted on the English sparrow memory bank and somehow was passed on to future generations saying, "Do not enter this area ever again." I've never understood the semantics of those birds.

The Rocks stayed at Greenlock for six years. During this time, their house was off-limits to all Greenlock staff, regardless of the weather. I decided it was time to put an addition on the Greenlock house. It would encompass the handicapped bathroom. Finally, we could have an office, bathroom, kitchen, and conference room with a sleeping loft. The Rocks were not happy with this plan, and they announced they were retiring to Maine, where they had built a house and barn and could spend their golden years with their horses.

The Parker/Healey Years (1998-2005)

Thus, began the Parker years. When we hired the next farm manager, we focused on farm care, not horse care. We interviewed and finally hired Al Parker, a butcher, who owned Parker's Meat Market in Seekonk, with his almost-wife Marge. Marge seemed happy with the idea, since I think she wanted him to spend less time hanging out in the store, and the farm would provide a way to occupy his time.

Al Parker had no horse experience but could feed the horses, and he excelled at using any kind of farm equipment you could ride on. They required Saturday afternoon until Monday morning off so they could ride their Harley-Davidsons all weekend, and ride they did, in full attire and to every event near and far. The Harley obsession eventually transformed itself into a Corvette obsession.

Al had three daughters. His youngest, Heather Healey, was married and had an infant daughter, Michaela. Al wanted his daughter and her family to live near them, so when an eight-acre parcel of land with a three-bedroom house that bordered Greenlock became available, we bought it together. I took the six acres of pasture and he took the two acres that included the house. I now had a seventeen-acre farm, and Al had his daughter as his neighbor and a grandson on the way.

Al had two helpers when he worked at Greenlock: John Deere and Bobcat. If a job involved his working with John or Bob, he could transform anything, and during his time at the farm, he undertook some major projects. There was a small land-locked swamp on the property, which, with the conservation committee's approval, Al and Bob turned into a beautiful pond that included a small island on which a weeping willow was planted. With the fill from this project, he built a bridge, complete with culverts so we could use it to take our riders on trail rides in our woods and fields around the property. Al loved moving big boulders. He moved four and five-hundred-pound rocks around in order to delineate parking lots and boundaries. He made a memorial rock garden where we placed a small rock with the name of each animal who has passed on after being a part of Greenlock. One of the most amazing projects Al undertook was later labeled "the aqueduct." Providing fresh water for horses was always a project. Early on each stall had its own water bucket, and each paddock had a big water trough. We used a hose connected to the water hydrant to fill the buckets and troughs daily. The first myth is that there is no hose manufactured, regardless, of what package labels and advertisements say that won't kink. I know I have tried them all. The second myth is, at least at Greenlock, no hose, even the longest I could find one hundred feet, has ever been long enough to meet all our needs; and they are always short by only a few feet, thus they are always two hoses attached to each other. Winter brings a host of water problems due to water freezing. Every morning all winter long we had to take frozen buckets, usually full of undrunk water, bang out the ice, refill with water from the hydrant and carry them back to the stall. This created years of my having tendinitis of my right elbow in the winter. We used the hose to fill the troughs, but then we had to drain the hose of every ounce of water so it would not freeze and be unusable the next day. Water was Sheila's and my job, and we hated it! Al Parker watched us do this thankless job, took pity on us, and built us the Greenlock aqueduct.

Al moved all our water troughs to corners of paddocks in order that two or three paddocks could share troughs. He came up with a design that gave all the horses day and night access to one of these troughs. This worked since our horses live in run-in sheds, not stalls. This eliminated buckets. Next, he installed three hard rubber/plastic hoses starting on the ceiling above the hydrant and running across the rafters to each separate trough. Each was slightly angled so water would always drain out of the hose completely into the trough. Another piece of six-foot hose had hose connectors on each end and could be connected to the hydrant and then to the hose that led to the tub that needed to be filled. Great solution, and finally we could eliminate hoses, buckets, and tendinitis. And in winter Al added heaters to the troughs. Brilliant!

However, with great solutions, other problems develop. If a hose was filling a trough, it usually took about two to five minutes, a perfect amount of time to do some other task like cleaning a paddock, and then moving a horse, and then, water was forgotten until someone saw a stream slowing meandering through the paddock.

This happened to many of us multiple times and often for multiple hours. Our solution was to hang a clip on the hydrant with a two-inch thick, twelve-inch long, very red ribbon on it. When tubs were being filled you clipped the ribbon on your body to remind you and others that the water was running. This for the most part solved the problem. Except, one day, Sheila had gone home to Providence wearing the ribbon. I was a phone call away, so the water was finally turned off.

Since Al and Marge owned Parker's Meat Market in Seekonk, RI they knew many Rehoboth residents. Therefore, it came as no surprise when one day a woman called Mrs. Z showed up, unannounced, in her vintage County Squire station wagon and found Sheila and me cleaning paddocks. She brusquely asked if we wanted about one hundred bales of hay. Of course, we did! "Get in the wagon and I'll take you to look at them!" she barked. We did and were driven over to her gated estate, which had an eight-car garage filled with vintage and expensive cars, an Olympic-sized swimming pool, and a house filled with every Hummel ever made. In the brief moments Sheila could quietly talk to me, she said she realized Mrs. Z had been a neighbor of her mother's on the East Side of Providence, and she had gone to their synagogue, and perhaps it was best if I kept a low profile, i.e., not talk. We were swept out to two awaiting golf carts. Mrs. Z drove one and Leonardo, her estate keeper, the other. Sheila rode with Mrs. Z, and I with Leonardo. We had a grand tour of her estate, complete with a second house for Leonardo and his family, a duck pond with exotic ducks, and endless flower and veggie gardens tended by Leonardo's wife. The estate also included an eight-stall state-of-the-art barn that contained three thoroughbred horses and a pony. Mrs. Z explained that the horses were failed racehorses that a close friend of hers, Patsy Meadow, sent to live on her estate. What a coincidence! Patsy had been one of my best friends years ago. I spent practically every weekend of my childhood at her house where we endlessly rode our horses together. What a relief! This connection gave me the necessary credentials to be allowed to talk.

Finally, we arrived at a hay field about to be cut and were asked if we wanted the hay when baled. It looked like the right kind of great hay, so we said yes, and she said it would be delivered when baled. Two days later, Leonardo showed up with about one hundred bales of hay, and, with our help, it was unloaded and put in our loft above the barn. Recently cut hay has always been a concern for me since it can, if baled too soon before it has fully dried, develop mold, heat up, get hot enough to start smoldering, and cause a fire. The next morning, I opened a few bales and felt enough heat to be concerned. When hay is baled, it is done by compressing ten or twelve sections, called leaves, into one bale. Sheila and I had to remove all the hay from the loft, open every bale, separate each of the leaves, place them on tarps, and spread it out all around the barn parking lot. Twice a day we had to turn each leaf over. What a nightmare, but luckily for us, it didn't rain and all the hay was saved and used!

Another adventure occurred when a neighbor, Chris, showed up one day and wanted my help in setting up a 501c3. He wanted to start an exotic animal educational program for kids. He lived down the street about a mile away from the farm and had acquired a collection of zedonks, camels, llamas, emus, and other exotic and unconventional animals. I agreed. The following week, Sheila and I went to his place. Once again, we were amazed and stunned by what we saw. The compound included a huge conventionally styled house with a two-story wire structure that enclosed one side of the house, complete with a tree or two. There were three huge metal buildings and a barn surrounded by at least ten big paddocks filled with animals. Our visit started in the house where we met Chris' wife and three-year-old daughter and two exotic cats: the bigger was about forty pounds and spotted and the other was smaller but equally exotic. They had a cat door off the living room that led out to the wire cage. Both cats seemed wary of us, as we were of them. The next room we went into had display cases of handmade painted lead soldiers, armies of them from every imaginable war, engaged in combat. Other cases had complete ensembles of orchestras made of lead players and their instruments. Not to be outdone, in another case, there were lead people in obscene and compromised sexual positions. Chris said he had made and painted them during his depressed years. He then took us to his basement where he had drawers full of more lead soldiers and people all painted and ready for what? He's never been sure what he would do with them. He told us for three years he did not talk with anyone; he just made and painted lead soldiers and people.

Next, we toured other buildings. One had been set up as an exhibition hall for his animals. The animals would be displayed on the ground floor and his future audiences would stand on the big balcony above. There was no handicapped access and no plumbing. Presently the building was used for storage, as were the other two huge buildings. All were filled with exotic wooden and wicker furniture and wooden carvings, some life sized. Chris explained that he and his wife traveled extensively with their daughter and her tutor and would go to remote villages to buy all their merchandise to bring home to sell. As of yet, they had not found a market for them.

In talking and seeing his place, it became apparent that Chris had many problems to resolve before his goal of creating an animal educational program could be realized. Foremost, the town was upset with him because his buildings were not up to code: he had no parking facilities or handicapped access. After a year or two of negotiations, he and his animals finally moved to Connecticut. His property in Rehoboth now lies abandoned.

About 2002, my husband Al and I gave our traditional Xmas party and we invited about twenty people including our vet Corrina. The following morning Corrina appeared and picked up Al for a road trip to an undisclosed location. They reappeared a couple of hours later, Corinna left, and Al revealed he now owned his own horse called Moose who would be arriving at Greenlock the next morning. Great another horse. Now my husband had never shown much interest in horses. However, apparently, Corrina wanted to save Moose, who was geriatric, because his owner, who was also geriatric, was moving to a nursing home, so Corrina secretly persuaded my husband to provide a retirement home for Moose.

The next day Moose appeared. He looked about fifty years old and was definitively circling the drain toward his eternity. He had very kind, but very sunken eyes. At one time he had been a white horse, but now he had sort of a yellow, gray cast to his rather mangy-looking coat. He moved as if every joint hurt, and he looked like he should be joining his previous owner in the nursing home, instead of coming to Hotel Greenlock for what was clearly hospice care. Corrina said not to worry, she would provide all his vet care and death benefits when the time came.

In late February of that year, Al and I were about to go on our winter vacation, this year to Cuba. The day before we left, it was snowing, and I did my morning check on the horses and all was well. I then went and did a last-minute errand. When I returned I found, Moose, lying dead in his paddock. No fanfare, no medical interventions, his time had come and he said, "I'm used up and done." From my perspective, that's a pretty perfect death.

An added benefit of Al living here was that he often brought home store goodies such as packages of Boar's Head hot dogs or Kielbasa to give to us. One late afternoon I was walking home at the end of the day with a couple of packages of hot dogs and my dogs, and suddenly two fire trucks with sirens and flashing lights came roaring down the driveway. They stopped when that saw me and said, "Where's the fire?" I said, "What fire?" "Greenlock called 911!" "No one here called 911," I replied. We were all somewhat baffled, and there was no fire. The driver of the fire truck then suggested that maybe we could all roast hot dogs together.

All was forgotten for a couple of days, until one night about two AM we got loud and persistent knocking on our front door. My husband got up to answer it and he was told by two policemen that Greenlock had called 911. The policemen had looked around the farm and had not found a problem, so were checking out domestic violence as a possible reason for the call. I was aroused to see if I were the victim, and it turned out the Parkers had also been checked out in case there had been domestic violence at the farm's house.

Two unexplained 911 calls needed further investigation. At the time the farm had one phone line with the same number in four different building locations. The unique characteristic of this was that the same phone number was located both at my house and the Greenlock house. This involved a transformer on a telephone phone on the road. Apparently, bees had decided that the transformer was the perfect home and it turned out they were setting off the 911 alerts. The electric company finally resolved the issue.

Al and Marge decided to sell their meat market and spend winters in the sunny south. This allowed his daughter, Heather Healey, and son-in-law, Michael, to move into the house for about a year and continue Al's mission of transforming the farm into a showpiece. The most major event that occurred during their tenancy was another water problem. It happened on a Saturday when the Healeys had their friends, Cathy and Joe St. George (who incidentally later became our farm manager) over for the afternoon. The hydrant in the barn broke, so there was no water.

Unfortunately, this occurred in January. The high temperature for the day was about twenty degrees and there were about eight to ten inches of frozen ground; global warming was not yet in vogue. Of course, the hydrant was submerged in the ground at least four feet. Therefore, the problem was four feet underground, and our barn floor was dirt. The solution involved digging up the floor so a person could get in the hole and fix the pipe. Luckily, the hydrant repair man was a neighbor and he told Michael he would return when an adequate size hole had been dug. No small task and Michael was not happy. In fact, he was "pissed" with what was now his job that had to be done that day, and he even refused his friend Joe's help. He found a jackhammer and went to work. About four hours later he called the pump repair man who had the pump fixed in about fifteen minutes. At the end of the day, we had water again.

In the early spring of 2003, I answered the phone and it was a farm twenty-five miles from us just south of Boston and they explained a long-distance rider, named Gene Glasscock, needed a place to stay and they thought I could provide for him and his two horses, both Tennessee Walkers. I knew nothing about long-distance riders and soon learned they are people who ride continuously to accomplish some extraordinary goal. In the 1980s Gene had ridden twelve hundred miles from the Arctic Circle to the Equator. Now at sixty-seven he was one-third of the way through a twenty-thousand-mile trip across the continental United States and was stopping in every state capital. My job was to care for him and his horses on his way to Providence, and then to find them their next set of accommodations.

Gene rode down Summer Street and arrived at Greenlock in the late afternoon. Since this was somewhat extraordinary, I invited Corrina our vet to join us for dinner that night. This turned out to be a fortunate move. Gene was concerned that one of his horses was lame and needed a vet, and both his horses needed new shoes. Gene ended up staying with us for three nights, and all his horse needs were taken care of with no charge. The lame horse could continue the journey for a stop or two, but would then be swapped out for a new horse. A group called the "The Long Distance Riders Guild" monitored Gene, his health, his progress, and his horses' health, and they could swap out his horses as needed.

Three days later Gene was ready to move on with his trip. His stop that day was the Rhode Island State Capitol. He was met at the RI state line by the Providence Mounted Police, and escorted to the capital, for the official signing of his capital visits. That night he and his horses stayed at the mounted police horse stable at Roger Williams Park, their next destination Hartford, CT, and then New Jersey. Gene's trip around the USA was also being used as a way of raising money to send students from Paraguay to a Christian school in Florida.

Gene had once been a teacher in Paraguay and had fallen in love with its people. Hence the ride was made for their cause.

The Bedard Years (2005-2010)

After the Parkers left, we hired Ray Bedard, a friend of one of our great volunteers. They both hung out at the Moose Lodge in Attleboro, RI, where Gary, the volunteer, with the pen name of "Nature Boy," was a World Wrestling Alliance wrestler. Ray was a Vietnam vet. Sheila and I did the interview and asked him about smoking and drinking. Both had been given up. He presented as a great find, and he came with his company truck, complete with parts and tools for maintenance work. He said his work hours were flexible, which suited us perfectly.

Ray and his wife, Donna, moved in with their Min Pin, a miniature version of a Doberman Pincher. All was great for the first year, but during the following years, nothing seemed to go right for him. First, they found a new home for the constantly barking Min Pin, who, if he got loose, ran away. Then Ray acquired a German Shepherd puppy he named Moo after a dog who had lived in his company in Vietnam. Moo was actually the calmest puppy I have ever met, but it turned out he had a congenital, undiagnosed, heart condition and he keeled over and died one day at a year old. So sad, but Ray was not done with dogs. He acquired another Shepherd, who at ten months, became the most aggressive dog I have ever witnessed. Donna, his wife, was terrified of the dog. We were all terrified of the dog. Ray tried to get the dog trained, but this did not seem to help and the dog became unsafe to have at Greenlock. We told Ray that the dog could not stay, and we suggested that he take a break from having a dog for a while.

Ray's next set of problems involved his daughter's having marital problems and needing a place to live with her two young children. Soon, they, too, moved into the small Greenlock house. Ray's grandson was a very responsible and likable eight-year-old. Ray taught him to use all the mowers and now he could do most of the mowing under Ray's watchful eye. Lastly, because the company he worked for was concerned about his interpretation of work flexibility, they put a tracker on his truck. Ray was devastated; he had lost all his freedom and was now an eight-to-five guy.

During Ray's stay with us, I had my first run-in with a pack of coyotes. It was late February. My house was by the road, about two-tenths of a mile from the barn. Every night at about 8:30, I would walk with my two dogs up to the barn to check the horses and give them nightly carrots. On this particular night, I stepped out on my deck and heard coyotes. I left the dogs at home, jumped into the car, drove to the barn, and in the field next to the Greenlock's driveway were eight coyotes. I gave the horses their carrots, drove home, and the coyotes were still there. The next night all was normal again, but the following night I got to the barn with the dogs, and while I was in the barn, the coyotes started howling again right outside the back of the barn. I called Ray to come out and assist my dogs and me on the walk home. He did, the coyotes stayed, but they did not bother us. At this point, I asked myself why didn't my dogs react? It was so odd.

Two nights later, I was walking with the dogs to the barn again, and with my flashlight, I could see coyote eyes in the field on the other side of the driveway. I gave carrots to the horses and returned home safely. I put my dogs in the dog yard and went back out to watch the coyotes. They crossed both fields and went to the big pond behind my house and disappeared. Later, when I put it all together, I realized they were interested in the goose and duck population that lived by the pond. They had no interest in me or my dogs, and, apparently, my dogs had no interest in them. This phenomenon of my dogs having no interest in coyotes had come up again on other occasions. A vet who researched coyotes on Prudence Island said to me once, "Coyotes are all around you. Your dogs know where they are and they know where your dogs are, but they respect each other."

During this time, the property on the far side of Greenlock went up for sale. It included a house, behind the house a swamp, and then twelve acres of field and four acres of wood, brook, and swamp. Once again, Al Parker wanted the house for yet another daughter, and I wanted the land to expand Greenlock. We bought the property, split it up and now I had a twenty-six-acre farm. When I first moved to Greenlock in its new location, this field had been a cornfield that was maintained by Dennis Mello, one of the nicest and most handsome men I have met. During the winter months, he spread all our manure on the field and we could use his field to ride in. Come spring, when he came to harrow, he also harrowed all our trails to make them easy to walk and ride on.

Unfortunately, his lease was not renewed, and when the owner died, his son took over the property. The son thought he could farm it. For four years, the son tried farming and, as time went on, the field came to look more and more like a cross between a landfill and a used car and equipment lot. I started planting trees along the property line to try to hide the rusting debris. When the property went up for sale, we bought it, split it, and cleaned up one-hundred-and-six used tires, forty-six car batteries, eight dead, old tractors (most without engines), two rusty house trailers, three dead vans, corroded farm equipment, and tools too numerous to mention, all dropped and forgotten where last used. The final item was a cow with a deformed leg, and her two-year-old bull, undersized due to malnutrition, along with at least a mile of random barbed wire fencing resting on the ground because the cows were hungry and pushed the posts down for their daily afternoon visit to Greenlock. There is no leash law in town, and this applies to cows also, so we adapted. And now I owned all of this including the cow and bull! The house was in even worse shape: rooms full to the ceiling with clothes, boxes, trash – you name it. It took about two months to clean up the property and get all the items appropriately disposed of. After the cleanup, I leased my new field out to Ben Monroe, who turned it into a hay field. Around the edge of the eleven-acre field, we put in an adventure trail where our riders can stop and play games while on their horse.

One of the bigger problems for us during the Ray years was his benign neglect of our equipment. While plowing, he backed the farm's pickup into a rock, denting the frame. He would joy ride in the ATV, he rarely maintained the mowers, tractor, and Bobcat. But he loved living at the farm and he truly believed he was an asset. And he was when he first came, but as time went by he got too comfortable and became lazy.

THE ST. GEORGE YEARS (2010–PRESENT)

On a one-out-of-ten scale, Joe's a twelve! He and his wife were friends of Heather Healey and were supposed to move into the Greenlock house five years earlier, but finances around a house mortgage made them back out, so we hired Ray. This time around they were ready to move in. Joe is the kind of guy who does not want or need to be supervised or told what and when to do it. Hard to believe, but l figured this out about two days after he moved in. His wife, Cathy, said to me, "It will take about two weeks and Joe will know when and what to do," and he did. Sheila and/or Kathy and I had always done morning stall clean up, but about a week after Joe moved in, the stalls were done before we even got to the farm. I told him he didn't have to do stalls, but he never stopped as he felt they were part of his job. I asked him what days he wanted off. His response was none! If they were to go out or be gone, they would let me know.

Joe was a jack of all trades. He had had numerous jobs before finding us and they had all prepared him for being here. Small engine repair – no problem, he could use and fix them all. Tractor and Bobcat maintenance – easy, and he had all our abused engines back humming within a month of being here. And with all this equipment, he transformed the farm into a showplace to be proud of. Often, I suggested to Joe that we should buy a new piece of equipment, and you would think I had insulted him. No, he could repair and make do with what we had. Joe did not like to spend money, and that included Greenlock's money.

Joe and Cathy loved the horses. They would often be found just sitting on a rock in the horses' paddock, holding a brush or mint, and just trying to be one with the herd. Joe took great care of the horses. He noticed small details about their behavior and when something was off, he'd mention it to me, even if he thought it was inconsequential. This helped us avert many horse health problems.

About two years after Joe arrived, we took an older mare, Mardi, on trial. She was a retired polo pony. The owner's daughter was a volunteer here and we felt we should at least try the horse because we really liked her and her family. They said they would bring Mardi to us so we could trial the horse as long as we needed to. Initially we thought this horse was pretty stiff and arthritic from her active polo life, but also, she was well trained. Mardi spent the night and as we always did with new horses, we left her halter on overnight in case there was an emergency.

The next morning, I was on my early morning bike ride and I got a phone call that Mardi had escaped and taken off up the hill with Joe in pursuit. I started back to Greenlock and about a mile from the farm, I found Mardi grazing on the side of the road. Cars had stopped and I exclaimed, "That's my horse!" I asked a man with a pickup truck to take my bike back to Greenlock and try to find Joe. I grabbed the horse by her halter and started walking her back to the farm. Mardi was being a bit fractious, and I had no lead rope, so I couldn't let the halter go to get my cell phone and call for help. It was a long walk, but we finally made it. There was no sign of Joe, and he, on principle, would not use a cell phone anyway. I didn't know how Mardi had escaped, so to be safe, I locked her in her stall, grabbed my bike, went home, and got ready for the day.

An hour later, when I returned, Joe had not realized she was back and in her stall. His relief was palpable. He told me she had pushed a gate open and run off (perhaps trying to get back home) and he had searched for two hours. A few days later we decided that Mardi was not a candidate for our program; she seemed so unhappy. We called the owner and they, apparently, really did not want her back. It took us two weeks to get them to agree to take her back.

Joe claimed he was not a rider. Once we took him on a visit to look at a potential new Greenlock horse. During the visit, we asked him to get on the horse. He did, but rested his heels, not the balls of his feet, but in the stirrups, and rode that way. Strange. And when commented on, he said he felt it was safer. Many months later on a trail ride, a friend was riding her horse with us. She had an unfortunate fall from her somewhat unruly horse and had to walk out to the road and be driven home. Joe drove the car to pick her up, said he would ride the horse home, and I should drive her home. Forty minutes later, Joe appeared on the horse looking like a pro with a smile on his face and with his feet planted properly in the stirrups.

Joe was at Greenlock during the Trump and Covid years. Our town, Rehoboth, resides in Massachusetts, a liberal state, but Rehoboth is actually a politically split community. Three of the farm's neighbors are Trump-conservative and Covid deniers. I had always loved my neighbors, and I had become very good friends with many of them. I had spent many hours socializing with them, but how do neighbors live in such harmony when they often have such different views on so many issues? My solution to this problem was to embrace it and engage in dialogue to try to understand their views, as well as my own. Joe was my mentor in this process. We spent many hours together, including long rides in trucks pulling trailers to acquire and return horses. Our discussions were all over the map, from gun control, to LBGTQ issues, to vaccines, to Hilary Clinton, and to Ukraine. I would ask him questions and learned that his answers were never predictable. My assumptions about how he would respond to each issue were wrong. For example, I asked about mass shootings and assault rifles. His answer was: we need to focus on the mental health crisis. I asked him about supporting Ukraine. His answer: we need to solve issues in this country first. LBGTQ was fine with him because it is an individual choice, but being "jabbed" was unacceptable, as was health care in general, at least, for him. I found this all fascinating, and I was developing an understanding of where our differences came from and acquiring some ability to actually laugh about them together.

Most recently on the Monday that Tucker Carlson was fired by FOX News, I was eating lunch at the picnic table by Joe's back door. During lunch, Joe came out of the house and said to me, "You can't even trust the news. The reporters lie! You can't even trust the news," he kept repeating. I agreed with him and thought maybe Joe had an epiphany.

Cathy, Joe's wife, is more of an independent, and she occasionally brought humor into our differences. One night we were having dinner, and she commented, "You'll never guess what Joe got in the mail today!" She was right. I would never have guessed: an eighty-day supply of dehydrated survival food. Yes, Joe was a survivalist and a bit of a hoarder for the future. But I knew if the fat really did hit the fire, he just might include me in his circle of friends.

During this time, I had an outdoor memorial event at the farm for my husband, who had recently died. Now, I come from a liberal family and my sister is ultra-liberal. She once told me she had no conservative friends. My thoughts were: how can we solve differences if we can't learn to laugh at them? My sister's daughter and her husband were staying at the farm overnight that night, and, apparently, after the event was over, they stayed up late into the night with Joe and Cathy, and, unbelievably, they talked politics. From all reports, they had a great evening and my niece still talks about it.

Joe is still with us today and he is still a twelve on a one-to-ten scale. I find I am very dependent on Joe as I fade into the decrepitude of old age. When Joe finally decides he has had enough of the farming life, it will be a sad day for Greenlock. The saying goes, "All employees are replaceable." I'm not so sure in this case.

CHAPTER VI

FRIENDSHIP

From the start, Sheila and I were very good friends. We often argued to the point of people thinking we weren't getting along, but these arguments always resulted in great outcomes, and even when arguing, our relationship was based on humor. But we are opposites in so many ways. Sheila is an extrovert, I'm an introvert; Sheila likes to travel, I like to stay home; Sheila is sensitive to how people feel, I'm oblivious; Sheila's polite; I've been described as irreverent. Sheila always wanted to spend money; I never wanted to spend money. This latter issue was the root of many of our arguments. Sheila's and my relationship was built around trust, respect, and laughter. We spent hours together, and all were memorable.

Sheila's skills included supervising all our employee relationship problems. When we had to talk to any employee about any sort of transgressions, it was Sheila's job, and she was masterful. An example is one of our barn managers, who lived on-site with his wife, was often spending the night away from the farm and sometimes had the Greenlock truck. Another employee often saw him with another woman who lived where the truck was parked overnight. Sheila and I met with the employee, and after Sheila had expressed her concerns, as no other person could, the individual thanked her for the feedback and reflected on how his behavior could be detrimental to Greenlock and perhaps many people around him.

When Sheila returned from her vacations, people would inevitably tell her of all my, and others' transgressions, and they would all be worked out. She was like a great organizational therapist.

I had skills, also, but of a very different nature. I'm a visionary, so if you need a problem be solved, I am the person to solve it – especially if it is a potentially costly problem. I could figure out how to solve it at almost no cost. I excelled at infrastructure. Buying tractors, mowers, and hay, and repairing driveways, roofs, and septic systems – all were easy for me. My second skill was finding people to work at any job that Greenlock needed to be done. Whether it was a computer person, a bookkeeper, or a way to plow snow, I was the person to make it happen.

One example was when Greenlock needed its riding arena, a building one hundred sixty feet by one hundred feet, painted (a task needed about every eight years). I found a local church group that volunteered to come for a day and paint the arena. They showed up with over one hundred people, including painters, a carpenter, and a staff to cook lunch for the entire group. The painting job was divided into four groups: one per side with a painting contractor in charge of each side. At the end of the day, we had a freshly painted arena. This same church has painted our arena twice.

Another project that had to be undertaken was to build a three-bay shed row for our expanding equipment needs. I persuaded the Dighton-Rehoboth High School to build this shed and they did. We paid for the materials but the labor was free. It took them two years since they could only come three days a week from one to three when they weren't on vacation, but the outcome was well worth the wait.

Sheila and I first met in 1984 at Gut Club, a monthly potluck dinner put on by a small group of friends living near each other. Every month's dinner was based on a different ethnic food. Then in 1986, a neighbor asked Sheila and me if we wanted to join a self-actualization women's group. She had invited about ten people. We went to two meetings. The first was an introduction and "getting to know you" event. The second was to investigate our personal future aspirations. It turned out this group of women had no aspirations beyond grandchildren and retirement travel; being an introvert, I waited until near the end to speak, and I talked of my dream to create a therapeutic riding center in Rehoboth. My future plans fascinated the group, and the rest of the meeting was a discussion of this future. The third meeting was about personal risk taking and included walking over hot coals. That focus proved too much for Sheila and me so we quit the group. But the group had done its job because it sowed the seeds of what was to become our future relationship, friendship, and successful business.

We had both had midlife horse crises, which resulted in each of us having recently acquired our own backyard horse, and we lived around the corner and a field away from each other. Thus, began our endless trail rides to the far corners of Rehoboth. During these rides, we had so many probable and improbable conversations about our lives, our families, and our aspirations. We discovered that we had both worked at the Fernald State School in Waltham, Massachusetts, at the same time. We even remembered many of the same clients, and that my mother, a medical student at Johns Hopkins, had been in Labrador at the Grenfell Mission, about the same time that her father, a dental student at the University of Maryland, had been there. We both grew up with moms who worked full time at their professions, during our childhoods, and we both had fathers die when we were ten years old.

Lastly, and perhaps most importantly, we had both been born in the '40s, so we were products of the '60s, and we lived through Vietnam, Woodstock, Haight/Ashbury, and drugs – in our case, weed. It should be no surprise that when medical marijuana became legal in Rhode Island, it became an inviting option. One day Sheila told me she had gotten a prescription for medical marijuana from her doctor. I thought nothing of it until about a year later when a parent of one of our clients asked if it might be a good option for her son who had a brain injury resulting from a car accident. I suggested she talk with Sheila. Later that same year, I noticed when she was here, my dog Tee-aka-Boo, had stolen a baggy from her car. I asked her what it was. Silence. Then, "You don't want to know," but I did want to know. "Half a cookie." Oh, yes, that kind of cookie! Now it was in my dog! Forty-five minutes passed. Nothing happened, and then *boom!* On our walk home, Tee-aka-Boo decided she had to go to sleep and kept lying down. Finally, I dragged her home and fed her, since I hoped it would get the drug absorbed. She slept well that night and the next day all was fine. Two weeks later, my husband found a front-page article in the *New York Sunday Times* entitled, "Danger of Marijuana in Dogs." He cut it out and sent it to Sheila.

One of our more improbable discussions occurred about religions. Sheila was brought up in the Jewish tradition and I had gone to a Unitarian church on rainy days in the winter, but it didn't take. When we were in the woods riding, I commented if I had to choose a religion, I would become Jewish. Then I revealed that my grandmother on my Dad's side, whom I had never met, was Jewish. Sheila asked what her maiden name was, and when I told her, she said it wasn't a Jewish name. Upon occasion, this issue came into our discussions, but it was never resolved until we found ourselves in Newport at a benefit polo match that supported Greenlock. It was an upscale tailgate event, and Sheila had invited some of her East Side friends. I started talking to a woman who was carrying a fabulous parasol that had kitsch hanging all around its fringe. She had bought it on a trip through France and Israel. Somehow, this discussion turned to my having a grandmother from France named Bernays/Béarnaise. She asked how it was spelled, and I replied, "Bernays." She said, now that's a Jewish name! Sheila was standing next to us, and she exclaimed, "Oh my God! You're Jewish! I always assumed it was spelled like the sauce!"

On another trail ride, I brought along a friend of mine, Mark Hutchinson, whom I had met many years earlier through my husband.

We had been to at least two of his weddings and he and I had planned other potential career moves together, which did not materialize. He was the Juvenile Division Director at The Justice Resource Institute, and I had him in mind to be one of the first new members of Greenlock's Board of Directors, which we were slowly going to build over time. Sheila needed to meet him and decide for herself. Mark was a horse person. He had grown up with horses on his mother's ranch, and he could and would ride any horse, regardless of its age and history. What better way was there to introduce him than on one of our trail rides? Mark rode Sultan, an Arab cross, that belonged to a friend of mine. This horse later became a wonderful Greenlock horse. We had a great ride, which actually turned into his interview, and by the end of the ride, Sheila suggested he become a Greenlock Board Member.

Over the years, Sheila and I had many experiences with horses that we hoped Greenlock could use because we liked them but ultimately failed the cut. We had horses that we already used but had quirks that we tried to fix. One such horse was Odin, who was one of the best lesson horses Greenlock has ever had, and I think the only horse that Sheila ever truly loved. Sheila often took him on trail rides, and he would not cross a stream without first refusing and then suddenly leaping over it. Sheila decided we were going to train Odin to walk through water, so off we went in our rubber boots, Odin in tow, to the stream on the farm property to solve this deficiency. After thirty minutes, we finally had Odin calmed, walking back and forth over the stream while we led him. We thought that was easy. Now Sheila got on Odin bareback and tried to cross the stream. He refused, so she asked again, and Odin once again leapt over the stream, but this time Sheila was propelled off his rump and fell in the stream on her back. It was all pretty funny and we still laugh about it today. Incidentally, this was the same stream where I had broken my ribs falling. It now has a bridge over it, sort of like "Bridge Over Troubled Water."

Mark often tried to help us solve our horse problems. As I said, he would ride anything, so we had him help with a horse called Magic that Sheila had acquired for us when she was vacationing on Cape Cod. Magic was the perfect size for our mission and had perfect movement with suspension. He moved like a dancer. Unfortunately, after about ten or fifteen minutes of work, Magic had had enough and no longer wanted to be ridden. Once he had made this decision, if you tried to ask him to work, he would start by backing up and refusing to move forward. If this didn't work he would start bucking until you stopped asking. Mark thought he could fix it.

After the first fifteen minutes, Mark had Magic looking like a dream horse and then, like a light switch, Magic started to back up. Mark decided if he wanted to walk backward that was fine, and around the ring they went in reverse. This led to Magic switching his tactics and bucking. Now Mark was riding a rodeo bronc around and around the ring, but having a blast, as only a handsome macho man can. Mark did not fix Magic that day. We were now done with the horse, but our trainer, Bruce, wanted to take him to a dressage barn in Rhode Island because the horse was so talented in his movement, and he, too, thought it could be fixed. We said "okay," thinking that was the last of this horse at Greenlock. Once again, we were wrong. Six months later, we were asked to immediately come get the intractable horse; they were done. Sheila took the horse trailer to pick up the horse while I stayed at Greenlock because we had afternoon lessons. About three o'clock, Sheila called on her return trip with Magic and said he had gotten out of his halter and was riding backwards in her trailer with his head sticking out over the back of the door. She was concerned he might jump out, so did I have any suggestions? I said, "Let him jump and just keep driving, as if you never noticed." He didn't jump and he ended up being given to a family who wanted a pet horse in their backyard barn. This horse was an example of something that had gone terribly wrong in his earlier life, resulting in his not easily trusting humans again.

Sheila and I were both happily married. Sheila and Bob had three children. Sheila called her husband Bobby, so I, obviously, also called him Bobby. One random day about ten years into my knowing them, Sheila told me that Bobby had just told her over the weekend that he always preferred to be called Bob! I totally understood this preference, since as a child I was called Edie, but I preferred Edith. From that day forth, he was Bob. Sheila adopted the Bob name for a time, but she slowly drifted back to Bobby. Bob was a businessman, who had been in the printing business, until he started a local company called Pure Beverage.

My husband, Al Darby, had four children, my stepchildren, who, it turns out, all loved me. Both our families became very involved with our Greenlock venture over the years. Al was a medical doctor who specialized in child psychiatry. Marsha, one of my husband's daughters, was one of our first volunteers at Palmer River. She was a graduate student at the University of Rhode Island, studying to become a speech pathologist. She came to Rehoboth late in the afternoon, volunteered, and then had dinner at our house. David, his youngest son, was living in Boston during the '90s. He spent many weekends with us helping out at Greenlock and taking riding lessons from Bruce. David went on to become an accomplished dressage rider. Al's grandson, Dan, who lived in Foxboro, MA, also spent many weekends with us, helping out at the farm and learning to ride. His better half, Alisa, is presently the Chairman of Greenlock's Board. Lastly, Al's other daughter, Liz, presently is a volunteer at Greenlock.

Sheila's family was likewise very involved. Her daughter, Wendy, who changed her name to Wensday, was a singer and performing artist, and she performed at many of our fundraisers over the years. Sheila's son, Todd, made Greenlock's first promotional video (and, incidentally, my great nephew, Matt, made our most recent promotional video). Her youngest daughter, Stephanie, was awfully involved during the '90s. She had a horse called Jazzy, was in Pony Club, and took lessons from Joan and Tom at Palmer River. During this time, Stephanie was always at Palmer River. It was sort of her second home, and years later, Jazzy briefly became a Greenlock horse.

Sheila was a permissive parent and she let Stephanie have occasional outdoor sleepovers with her friends at Palmer River. On one such sleepover, Stephanie brought along her five six-week-old kittens to sleep in the tent with her and her friends. The next day, only four kittens could be accounted for; one was missing. Everyone searched to no avail. The remaining kittens went home. Two days passed. No kitten turned up, so the episode was thought closed. The next day, Sheila and I went to Fisher Feeds, about two miles away, to get supplies. As we left the store, we heard a faint meowing from the truck engine. Steve Fisher opened the hood of the truck, and there, sitting on the carburetor, was the kitten. It had used up one of its nine lives in this adventure.

Sheila and Bob and Al and I even traveled together. We made two or three trips to a working ranch in Roy, New Mexico; we did a rafting camping trip down the Grand Canyon from Lake Powell to Lake Mead; and we did a road trip around Idaho and through Glacier National Park ending in Missoula, Montana. On this trip, we met a well-known Indian guide named Curley Bear. Curley Bear's mission as a tour guide was to give his white tourists a realistic, yet somewhat outrageous, tour of the injustice imposed by our forefathers. A few of our stops included a school where our forefathers had abused Indian children and a cliff where our forefathers had run buffalo off and then shot them for sport. It felt like an immersion tour.

We also partied together. The most memorable was my fiftieth birthday. I was born on Halloween, so of course, it was a costume party. The party was at Sheila's house and about forty people came. Al and I came a little late so we could make a grand entrance after everyone else had arrived. We transformed ourselves into a horse. Al was the front legs and head and I was the hind legs and body. We had a huge gray papier mache horse head mask which Al controlled, and a gray horse blanket covered us, complete with mane and tail. We trotted into the party, stopped, paused, and then I raised the horse's bum and tail, and pooped out twenty golf balls. Then we walked to the bar. It was a great and memorable party.

Another great party occurred in the late '90s. Friday night we had our then-annual cocktail party at the Hi Hat in Providence. I had asked Lisa Powers, our first riding instructor, to visit for the weekend. She was now living in South Carolina. She came and on the Saturday night after the fundraiser, we went to Sheila's house for dinner. Also invited were Carol and Howie Horsmen because their son Ben had ridden with Lisa at Palmer River. Now Carol, who has never touched liquor in her entire life may be the funniest and most outrageous person I know. She is the only person I know who comes into a party and people assume she has been drinking or is on drugs; not so!

It happened to be Kentucky Derby Saturday, and a huge, state-of-the-art back then, fifty-inch TV was on the wall of the master bedroom. Sheila and Bobby were lying on the bed watching the Derby so immediately Carol jumped on top of Bobby and rolled to the middle of the bed between them. Finally, the rest of us all piled on the bed to watch the Derby. Dinner followed and then we settled in their sunken living room. Carol asked where the bathroom was and Sheila told her. Carol immediately came back and asked what all the buttons were for on the toilet. Sheila said, "It's a bidet." Now a bidet is sort of like using mouthwash after you brush your teeth. It tingles and puckers your mouth. Carol asked, "What's a bidet?" Sheila then took Carol for a bidet lesson. After a few minutes, Sheila returned. Five minutes, then ten minutes pass - no Carol. Finally, Carol came prancing into the room sort of squealing, and had a somewhat quizzical expression on her face. She exclaimed, "Ow-ee-oh-*wow*, the toilet had water flowing from every direction. I never knew I had all those nooks and crannies." Then I asked, "What took so long?" And Carol replied, "I pushed every button, then I got up to see what was happening down there, and water was going everywhere so I sat down again. When it finally stopped, I had to dry off and then clean the bathroom." Of course, we all burst out laughing!

During our years together, Sheila and I always felt like we could and should do much of the farm work. We bought a chain saw, a weed whacker, and numerous mowers, all of which we could never start when we needed to use them. Over the years, I constantly said to Sheila, "If I were to have an affair, it would be with a small engine mechanic!" We created huge burn piles of brush and then burned them with permission from the fire department. One of our big problems was dust. The moment our indoor or outdoor arenas dry out, they turn into great clouds of dust whenever horses walk on them. Nothing about this problem was healthy for horses or humans. We solved much of the indoor arena's dust problem by putting in a dug well and setting up a sprinkler. This worked well, except in winter when it froze, or in summer when we had a drought and the well went dry. The outdoor arena's footing was sand and on hot summer days we called it "The Beach." If it was at all windy, it became a dust bowl. Sheila investigated the problem. The first solution was used motor oil, often used on dirt roads. This solution was rejected due to the environmental impact. Sheila then discovered we could buy forty-pound bags containing small white pellets, which would expand with water when wet and slowly release the water as they dried. It seemed like the perfect solution. They were used in nurseries to keep plants constantly moist. All we had to do was spread one hundred bags of these pellets on "The Beach" before a light rain.

It took all day to spread and rake, but with some volunteer help, we accomplished the job. We thought we had picked the perfect day. A light rain was predicted overnight, and the pellets would fill with water and release the moisture back into the footing. That night the light rain turned into a deluge, and over an inch fell. The next morning, we went up to the arena and it was covered in clumps of clear gelatinous goo. Every pellet had burst open from too much water. Our solution had failed and the arena was unusable until it fully dried out.

Another somewhat random adventure, occurred when we were asked by one of our volunteers if we could bring a horse into Providence because her neighbor and friend were making a movie called *Breakfast With Curtis* and they needed a horse for one of the scenes.

We thought the idea was great. On the appointed Tuesday morning we loaded a larger chestnut Quarter Horse named Niki into our trailer and headed into the city. When we arrived, we unloaded Niki, saddled him up, and led him onto the movie set. Immediately we realized that the set was not horse-friendly. There were two huge cameras suspended in the air on mounts that kept moving, there were narrow sidewalks with uncut grass on each side that Niki had to walk down without eating, there was an actor who was to ride Niki, but who had no horse experience, and lastly it was trash pick-up day in Providence, and everyone's trash was out in three different recycling containers to be empty by three different trucks, that seemed not to notice or care that it was a movie set with a horse on it. Sheila and I were sure that disaster was going to strike at any moment.

The actual filming involved a fantasy scene in which an elderly woman named Sadie had a dream, in which she had received a phone call from Tommy Lee Jones asking her to go on a cattle drive with him. In the scene, Sadie was to run out of her house, and down the driveway to the sidewalk where Tommy Lee Jones was riding by on his horse. Sadie was yelling, "It's Tommy Lee Jones, it's Tommy Lee Jones, wait, I'm going on a cattle drive with you." And then she tried to jump on the back of the horse with Tommy Lee Jones. The film director had us repeat this scene at least twenty-five times. Between the grass that Niki wanted to eat, the garbage trucks that randomly appeared, the actors doing something wrong, and the cameras being in the wrong place, we did retake after retake. They finally got the scene they wanted, and Niki was a star that day in so many ways.

The movie was produced in 2011 and written, directed, and filmed by Laura Colella. The only professional actor in the movie was Aaron Jungels (Tommy Lee Jones). All the other actors, including the director and professional actor, are the people who actually lived in the three-family house adjacent to the one-family house in the heart of Providence where the filming took place. Sheila and I went to the movie's opening night. It was a great movie. In the credits we are listed as "The Horse Wranglers," and Niki was given credit for his sterling performance.

    Since Greenlock is a non-profit, it has a Board of Directors running it. From the beginning, Sheila and I held the two most important positions on the Board. Sheila was the Chairperson of the Board, and I was the President of the Board. Our Board of about eleven people was primarily responsible for fundraising and/or knowing where the money was and going after it. It was only after Sheila, and I were getting older that we realized we needed a Board that was really going to run Greenlock. This change proved challenging. Sheila, then the present chair, was, in theory retiring, so we selected a new chairperson, Susan Potter. Her charge was to start turning the Board into a responsible leadership body. Within two years, she had transformed the Board into a group of people who now governed Greenlock. She then set up a retreat for the Board, with pricey consultants, to get the Board to function as a group and to design the future of Greenlock. It was a wonderful day, with the required group processing and bonding. The consultants then sent us a great comprehensive summary. They suggested it would be best for the organization if, like Sheila, I left the organization. Now, that's a problem. I live at the farm, and I own the farm, I was planning to live there until I'm carted off to a nursing home. Greenlock would have to slowly ignore me, or shelve me, or live with my presence. Susan was a great chairperson. Unfortunately, she insisted that she was going to retire after four years, and a new chairman would have to be found.

    I found another great new chairperson by accident who was young, energetic, and could take Greenlock into the future that Susan had designed. It all came about because Dan, my husband's grandson, came down to visit us and the farm regularly. On one such occasion I was talking with his better half, Alisa, about Greenlock and I suggested she might want to be on the board. Of course, she did, and her expertise was in Marketing and Data & Analytics at a top tier consulting firm. Shortly after Susan resigned, Alisa became our new chairperson.

She brought with her a young and accomplished Certified Public Accountant, who became our new treasurer, and a website design specialist, who upgraded our website. Slowly Greenlock began embracing technology and entering the twenty-first century. The Board is now charged with finding a new Executive Director, who can carry Greenlock into the future, as I fade into my final green pasture.

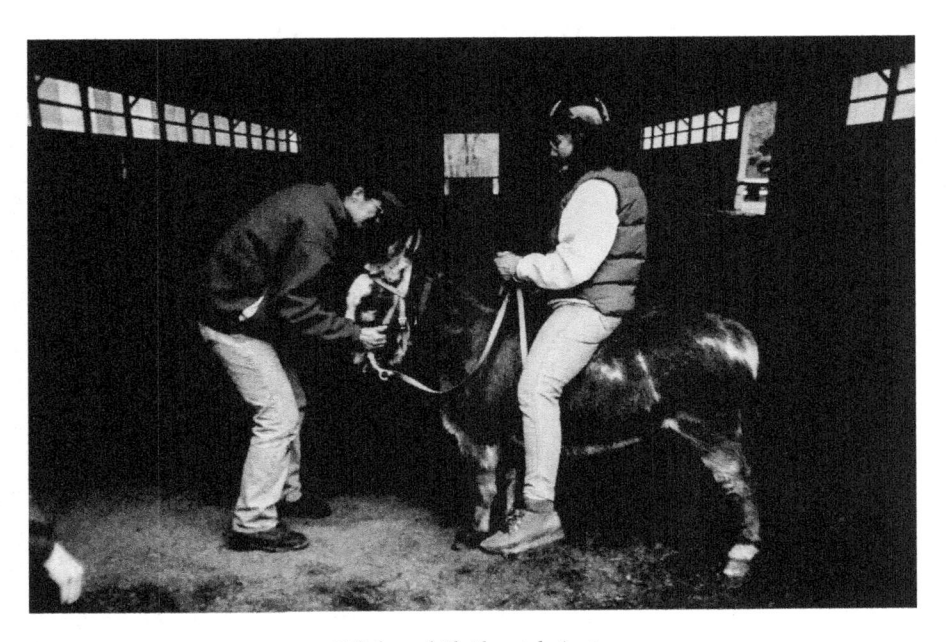

Edith and Sheila with Amigo

CHAPTER VII

HIPPOTHERAPY

My knowledge and adventure into riding for the disabled really started with my friend and mentor, Marge Kittridge, who ran Windrush Farm in Boxboro, MA, which was an established therapeutic riding center, and with Liz Baker, a physical therapist who was a colleague of mine at my real job, that paid real money, that I was trying to give up. Liz had an interest in learning about hippotherapy and had recently gone on a trip to Germany, which was where this new therapy using horses had its beginning.

So, what is hippotherapy and how does it differ from therapeutic riding? The simple answer is that in hippotherapy a licensed physical, occupational, or speech therapist is providing therapy on a moving surface (the horse) to clients. In therapeutic riding, an instructor is teaching people with disabilities how to ride a horse for fun and recreation.

The following was written by Liz Baker, RPT, HPCS in 1998, and it magnificently explains what we and hippotherapy are all about.

"Hippotherapy is a tool used by our therapist to improve rider's movement control, such as posture, mobility, balance, and coordination. In hippotherapy, the natural rhythmic movement of the horse is used to stimulate the rider's autonomic balance and postural responses. The walking horse causes the *normal rider to react with movements at the trunk and hips that are very similar to normal human walking.*

Many people with abnormal movement never experience this pattern of movement on their own, so they do not know what walking "feels" like; the horse provides this.

At Greenlock, the therapist does an initial evaluation to determine the rider's abilities and needs. The rider with a disability may have abnormal muscle tension or tone, decreased joint flexibility, decreased balance, and postural control. The therapist selects the appropriate horse and equipment after determining what the goals will be. These goals might include improvements in head control, coordination of breathing with swallow and vocalization, better upper body control to allow improved use of hands, improved trunk balance, independent sitting balance on a moving surface, and improved walking through better balance and control of legs.

Riders typically have hippotherapy sessions once a week. Safety and support are provided to each rider by having a horse leader/handler, a therapist directing the session, and a volunteer side walker assisting the therapist with the rider.

The rider's activities during the therapy session vary according to age and ability. Often, alternative positions are used to encourage organization and relaxation of the brain and body. Lying on the back of the horse encourages relaxation of spasticity, but also provides a strong sense of midline or "center" as the horse has a clear midline to his body that the rider can feel underneath him. With a rider lying either lengthwise or across the horse on their stomach in "prone" positions, they are encouraged to lift their head, to visually track people and objects, to relax muscles not needed, to sense their midline, and to begin to push away from the support surface-resisting gravity. Sitting facing backward refines the ability to sit up, maintaining balance against gravity. Weight-bearing on hands helps strengthen the upper body and promotes the ability to protect the face against falls.

Soon, the rider may truly focus on sitting facing forward without always having to hold on for balance. From here the therapist and rider may work towards more improved balance, body control, and sensory processing through other developmental positions, such as kneeling on the horse or actually standing on a walking horse. This is serious strengthening, balance, and posture training for riders, leading them towards much better movement skills off the horse, and it is "off the horse" where each rider's function truly lies in making day-to-day life movement, easier and more efficient."

Many riders at Greenlock progress out of hippotherapy and into recreational riding (therapeutic riding), where the focus becomes learning to ride independently, controlling this big, but gentle animal under the direction of a riding instructor. When we started Greenlock, it was imperative that we find both riding instructors and licensed therapists in order to provide these services. This proved easier than expected and over the years we have usually had about three licensed riding instructors and around eight per diem therapists at any given time. Our therapists and instructors have been fabulous, and along with our horses, are the heart of our program.

Therapists are usually very serious people who are obsessed with being licensed and being regulated by various agencies and organizations, with each discipline having its own set of rules and regulations and its own national organization, none of them overlapping. Additionally, over the years, these agencies' regulations slowly become stricter. As Greenlock was evolving, so was a grassroots organization called North American Riding for the Handicapped (later to become the Professional Association of Therapeutic Riding International) which was soon to become the regulatory agency for therapeutic riding centers. This organization added the requirement that therapeutic riding instructors must be licensed and later, that centers must be accredited. Over the years, the criterion for licensing of instructors became much harder, and much more restrictive as did the standards for accreditation. Initially Greenlock embraced both these requirements. But as the years have passed, these requirements have become mired in detail, and very pricey to attain, with no obvious benefits to our center, or to potential instructors who might choose to work here.

Additionally, and perhaps unfortunately, another grass roots national organization was forming, calling itself The American Hippotherapy Association, AHA – hippo being a Greek word for horse. This group instituted yet another set of standards for training therapists and conducting hippotherapy sessions at therapeutic riding centers. Then, in 1996 the Health Insurance Portability and Accountability Act (HIPPA) were enacted. All these developments had a major impact and influence on the evolution of Greenlock.

Lisa, our instructor, pushed Sheila and me to get our therapeutic licenses during our second year of operation. All this required at that time was to do a thirty-minute video of each of us teaching two disabled riders, and we got our license. If we had had to meet the standards of today's test, neither one of us could pass, so age has its advantages. As standards changed, we were always grandfathered in, although now, in addition, we have to take twenty educational hours and pass a written test to renew these licenses. The standards for becoming a licensed therapeutic riding instructor today are very expensive and your skill set must go far beyond what I feel you need to know to be a skilled instructor. However, the nature of group dynamics in organizations is that over time, they tighten their boundaries and make their requirements more and more rigid.

An example of how these regulatory rules affected our evolution is that when we started Greenlock, riders were people who rode on a horse with us by their side, sort of an obvious concept, and it did not matter if they rode the horse with a riding instructor or a therapist. Today we have "clients," no longer called riders, who are on a "moving dynamic surface," no longer called a horse. The horse has become just like a great big therapy ball. Luckily, if you are in therapeutic riding, you still remain a rider on a horse. This change in terminology came about because PTs, OTs, and SLPs, are really part of the larger medical community, and third-party billing is where the money is. Insurance will not pay for someone to ride a horse, but they will pay for a client to receive therapy on a moving dynamic surface, just don't mention it's a horse. In spite of the fact that Greenlock prides itself in not doing third-party billing, our therapists still take this therapy model very seriously and it is reflected in their client progress notes.

A progress note is a note written at the end of each therapy session that summarizes how the client is progressing towards a set of goals that was established at their semi-annual off (horse) assessment. When Greenlock started, progress notes did not exist, but as our regulatory agencies evolved, so did the need for progress notes. Every medical practice and special education programs in schools have them and so do we, volumes of them, rarely to be read again, and all kept under secure lock and key. In the early days, a progress note could mention the word horse, or even the name of a horse that a person was on, or even that the rider might have hugged the horse, or perhaps patted the horse, or even said his first word from the back of a horse. Not today: neither a horse nor its name is allowed in such a note.

Over the years, wonderful therapists have come and gone. In the early years, we had many PTs, and in our present years, many OTs. We have had the same speech therapist, Elizabeth Morley, for twenty-five years, and she is still with us today. Remarkably, she has one rider who has had her services for all twenty-five years. The therapists who come to work here often start as volunteers and then want to get more involved. Since Liz Baker was one of the founders of AHA, she was also instrumental in setting up their training curriculum, which included two, four-day workshops, "Introduction to Hippotherapy," and "Level Two Treatment Skills." While Liz Baker worked for us, she recruited a physical therapist, Mary Helene Chaplin, who followed in her footsteps and became part of the AHA faculty. As early as 1994, Greenlock started offering these courses at Greenlock and we still offer them today. We require all our therapists to attend at least the introductory workshop in order to work for us; most attend both workshops. An added advantage of teaching these courses is that therapists come to us from all over the country to attend these workshops. Some even come from foreign countries, and it's a great way to learn how different places provide their services.

When children come to Greenlock and receive hippotherapy, they often do not even know they are in therapy, because for them, all that really matters is that they are riding a horse, and this makes most children very happy. At the beginning of Greenlock, and for about ten years, we easily found physical therapists but occupational therapists were impossible to find. The next ten years we had a mix of therapy types, but in the last ten years, physical therapists have been impossible to find, and we have lots of occupational therapists.

So, what do PTS, OTS and SLPS actually try to achieve for these children on this horse? In the case of speech therapy, it is pretty clear, they work on communication. This could mean using sign language, or using a communication device, or making actual sounds using the mouth, tongue, throat, and breath control, to teach and control their speech. The horse's movement actually seems to encourage vocalizations, so the horse helps with the speech therapy.

In the case of physical therapy and occupational therapy, the question of which therapy can achieve the therapy goals is murky. I think of them as a continuum with PTs (who focus on muscles and joints moving properly) on one end and OTs (who focus on how sensory input makes us move functionally) on the other end. On this continuum, it seems like OT can flow into the PT purview, more easily and further, than PT can flow into the OT purview.

When Greenlock first started, I had little understanding of what OTs actually do. I was told they did sensory integration which meant nothing to me, and the word "occupational" offered no clue. Over the years I have come to realize that OTs feel that they are trained to meet most, if not all, functional needs of people with disabilities. With few exceptions, all the clients who ride at Greenlock presently could continue in hippotherapy with an OT. This includes clients with sensory problems, balance issues, high or low body tone problems, motor planning problems, emotional behavioral problems, and speech problems. The downside of OTs is that they are rarely ready to move any of their clients into a riding lesson program, for they can always find more goals to work on. This especially becomes a concern because no one knows how much the dynamic moving surface of the (dare we say horse) contributes to any outcomes. Perhaps the horse and their movement are actually doing much of the work, and the therapist is just an adjunct.

For over the thirty years, I have been involved with watching therapists provide therapy on a moving horse, and one question has always nagged at me. How much of the change in a client is because of the horse's movement, and how necessary is an actual credentialed therapist? Certainly, it is a provocative question but a relatively easy question to study. With research design in mind, I suggest a study be done in which about a dozen clients come to twelve consecutive weekly sessions. Every other session is run by either a registered therapist or a person without credentials, perhaps a riding instructor or a competent adult. A measurable five-minute pre- and post-test is administered on some dimension of their need, i.e. balance, hopping on one foot, walking, stair climbing, drawing, attention span, and following three-step commands. Examples of testing might be walking ten feet without stepping off a line, writing their name on a piece of paper, following in the correct order a set of instructions, or jumping ten times. A study client would ride on the same horse that met their physical needs each session. All sessions would be done at walk for thirty minutes in a prescribed area. The therapist/competent adult would choose the activities done during the thirty-minute ride. The outcome of this study would be interesting and perhaps a game changer.

Toby (horse) with Zach, client, and MH Chaplin, therapist

CHAPTER VIII

CLIENTS

Hundreds of people have come to our center over the years, and there are many testimonials to the changes our horses and staff have made to make their lives better. There were also so many memorable moments, some edifying, some funny, and all worthy of sharing. Greenlock never had to advertise for clients. From the beginning, people wanted our services and we always seemed to have a waiting list. People came in all ages and over the years, I think Greenlock has served every possible diagnosis, even extremely rare ones. We have served as many as one hundred and forty riders a week when we have had the right combination of instructors, therapists, and horses. Every time a news story was written about us, we knew that the phone would be ringing off the hook because even more people would want our services. A small number of our riders who started at Palmer River are still with us today.

People with disabilities really are just people, most with enormous, funny personalities who embraced our program with enthusiasm. And we embraced them. They came to Greenlock in all shapes and sizes, from two-year-olds who need to learn to walk, sit, balance, and talk, to kids who may not be able to use their hands or legs properly, to kids with no attention span, or very hyperactive behavior. Then there are kids with autism, cerebral palsy, Down syndrome, Prader-Willi syndrome, spina bifida, and teens with head injuries, traumatic brain injury, muscular dystrophy, and epilepsy, to mention just a few.

Ben started in hippotherapy when he was three years old with Liz Baker. Ben had cerebral palsy and was cute and very verbal. He rode with us for fifteen years. Ben was our poster child for many years with the blessing of his parents. If someone asked us to do a demonstration of what we do, Ben was our go-to child. Ben was also a movie buff. He knew almost every movie, who was in it, when it was made, etc. He would have won a movie trivia contest in a minute. Ben also had an amazing sense of humor, and when he was eighteen, he began a career as a successful comic at The Comedy Connection, a local comedy club. Ben also had a sense of adventure when he rode. If a horse did something odd, like shy at something, Ben would gather his composure and turn the spook into a story. One day he was riding Mosa, our neurotic Paso Fino, whom Ben loved since Mosa gave him independence. On this particular day, Mosa had a strange incident where he started to spin when we exited the woods outside the arena. I grabbed Ben off the horse, and once off, Mosa stopped and turned to us as if to say, "What just happened?" Ben said, "I think he has a poltergeist, like in the movie." It turned out Mosa was having a seizure. We had seen him do this odd behavior once before in the paddock, so we talked to our vet about it. She prescribed phenobarbital, a seizure drug. Luckily for us he relished eating his twenty pills a day and we never saw him do it again.

Ben was in fifth grade in 1995 when he wrote a composition for school called "Learning to Ride," and he got an A on this assignment. Here is his composition:

When I was about six years old, I started taking riding lessons to learn how to ride a horse. When I first started riding horses, I needed a leader and two side walkers. A physical therapist named Liz Baker sat behind me (back riding) when I first started because I couldn't (sic) hold my head up. She also did exercises with me to help me learn how to sit up on the horse. As the years went by, I improved. Here's how.

A few years later I no longer needed Liz to work with me. I only needed two sidewalks (sic) and a leader because I was bigger and stronger and able to sit up straight and hold my head up. I used different kinds of saddles over the years. Some of the saddles I used were an English saddle or a Western saddle.

Some of the things I did on the horse were trotting, around the world, kneeling, standing on the horse, while the horse was walking, and cantering. Some of the horses I rode over the years are Shah, Budweiser, Sulton, Spot, and my favorite that I always ride every week is Mosa.

When I was in third or fourth grade I started riding on my own without a sidewalk (sic) or leader. When I ride alone I steered the horse using the reins. I tell the horse which way to go by pulling on the left or the right rein, if I want the horse to stop, I just pull back on the reins.

I have been in many horse shows and demonstrations over the past few years. Some of the things I have to do on a horse show is sit up straight look through the horse's, ears, steer correctly and not get too close or bump into any other horses. Some other things I have to is to is the obstacle course. Then you line up and get your ribbons. You either come in 6th place, 5th place, 4th place, 3rd place, 2nd place or 1st place. The color of the ribbon tells you what place you came in.

I enjoy riding every week because the people there are helpful and always willing to answer questions. I feel very secure that I am able to ride on my own. I feel proud that I am able to ride a horse.

Although Ben stopped riding after his graduation from high school, he and his family remain close friends.

∞

*Ben Horsman's first ride with Liz Baker, therapist,
back riding with David Darby, sidewalker at Palmer River*

John was an autistic teenager who had ridden with us for about five years. He was nonverbal, had many issues with repetitive movements with his hands, and we were told he was a major behavior problem. At Greenlock, when he was on a horse, we never witnessed any behavioral outbursts. When he started riding with us, he was receiving hippotherapy with our occupational therapist, and about two years later he was moved to therapeutic riding, where he rode in a saddle for the first time. We were working with him doing exercises with his arms and up-downs in the saddle, pretty basic stuff. I was his instructor and felt I was getting no place; he was just being given a pony ride, and I wondered what his mom thought. At the end of one of our sessions, I sat down with her and suggested that they were not getting their money's worth because I was not making any progress with my teaching attempts. She looked at me and told me "The day John rides is the best day of our week. After he rides, he sleeps the whole night, he remains calm for twenty-four to forty-eight hours, and the night of the day he rides is the only night in a week we can go out to dinner because he calmly sits there eating." That's the power of the horse!

 Lisa had Prader-Willi syndrome. She started in therapeutic riding at about eight years of age when we were still at Palmer River and remained with us for another twenty years. One of the symptoms of this diagnosis is unmanageable weight gain and Lisa was short and stout. But we loved her, and over the years, with Sheila's help, she became a pretty good rider. Back then we even had a few riders whom we taught to canter. We had three horses we could use to teach canter: An Appaloosa, called Beringer, who was a retired event horse, had the most balanced, slow, and smoothest canter that any horse could have; a Missouri fox-trotter, called Blue, whose natural gait became a very smooth canter that he just progressed into by asking for a faster trot; and another Appaloosa called Arthur, whom you could put on a lunge line and control the canter by just asking for it verbally. Lisa often rode in a group with another of our riders, Caren, who was in our original riding group at Palmer River. She was developmentally delayed and remained riding with us for another twenty-four years. She also progressed, under Sheila's guidance, to learn to canter. Often, these two would go on small trail rides together. At this time, each horse had a volunteer or instructor with them, whose job was to help them with the horse. Whenever this person made a suggestion to Caren, Lisa was always quick to tell Caren what she was doing wrong. And then she would start bossing Caren around and correcting her based on what the instructor had said, but Caren never seemed to mind. One day we were walking through the woods and I was with Caren's horse and Kathy Darowski was with Lisa's horse. About three weeks earlier, sadly, my golden retriever called Spencer had been put to sleep due to bone cancer. Well, we were walking through the woods and Caren asked me, "Where's Spencer?" and before I could answer, I heard Lisa saying in a booming voice, "Spencer's dead, Caren. Spencer's dead. Spencer died, Caren. Didn't you know Spencer died?"

All Kathy and I could do was break out laughing. Caren seemed unfazed by Lisa and told me how sorry she was.

Marjorie, the wife of the Rhode Island governor, was, by far, our most famous rider. She had had an unfortunate accident when she was hit by a car while jogging. Prior to this accident, she and her husband, Bruce, had both been avid riders in Virginia, where they owned and fox-hunted their horses, John Riggins, and Refrigerator Perry. Their plan was for Marjorie to ride with us under supervision, help with her rehabilitation, see how it went, and if she still wanted to continue riding, they would donate both their horses, sight unseen by us, in order for Marjorie to resume riding on her own horse. She loved coming to Greenlock and rode a horse called Beringer. She was our only rider who ever jumped at our facility, and admittedly they were very low jumps. One day her two beautiful and shiny horses arrived at Greenlock, and they were huge – sixteen and seventeen hands tall. (Horses have their own standard of measurement: a hand is four inches, and you measure from the bottom of the front hoof to the top of the horse's withers, which is at the base of the horse's mane). Both horses were far bigger than anything we had ever had before. John Riggins did not take to our quiet life, so we leased him out to our old barn managers, Tom and Joan, as an event horse, where he loved his job. Refrigerator Perry had been Marjorie's horse. He stayed at our farm, and Marjorie continued to ride him for two more years. There were so many reasons to love Marjorie. She was witty, funny, and just loved being at Greenlock.

Andrew Bateson, a funny and cute six-year-old, also rode with us. He was recovering from a rare but serious case of bacterial meningitis, which was diagnosed at Rhode Island Hospital by an emergency room physician, a Dr. Linakas – whose son, coincidentally, had been with us for many years. As a result of his disease, both of Andrew's legs had been amputated below the knee and he was fitted with artificial prostheses. Soon after this occurred, Andrew was referred to us to work on strength training and learning that a prosthesis was no big deal.

His therapist was Sue Fisk and what a perfect match they were! Andrew usually arrived wearing sweatpants and most of our riders rode on a soft pad, not a saddle, so they did not have stirrups. During one of Andrew's early rides, unnoticed by Sue, one of his prostheses detached and slid off. This was hidden by his sweat pants and it landed on the ground. Andrew calmly said to Sue, "Can you please pick up my leg and put it back on?" From this point on, the loss of a leg became a running joke between Andrew and Sue. Actually, it turned out that the buttons that released the legs were on the inside and outside of the knee, so riding triggered the releases. Future revisions of his prostheses had to consider location based on Andrew's activities. A book was written about Andrew's experience by local writer, Mark Patinkin, called *Up and Running*, and his Greenlock experience is mentioned in this book.

Seth came to Greenlock in 1991 at age eighteen after having sustained a traumatic brain injury from an automobile accident. After the accident he was in a coma for about eight months. The accident resulted in his being in a wheelchair and having to use a communication device that he could type into, which became his voice. To some extent he could also use sign language. He came to us as part of his rehabilitation. Liz Baker was his first therapist, and later he moved on to seeing Mary Helene Chaplin, aka MH. During his time here he rode Beringer, Pippen, and Rosebud. Seth came two times per week. Seeing Seth drive up to Greenlock was always a pleasure, his smile was infectious, and he loved to tease and gently provoke his therapists. He used our wheelchair ramp to mount the horse. After he is on the ramp, his horse is led onto the ramp. His therapist would stand him up and pivot him around so he could sit on the saddle, and then the therapist with the assistance of the sidewalker would lift his leg over the horse's neck so he was astride the horse.

Seth was a very handsome and savvy young man who would often tease his therapy team during his sessions, especially MH. During the summer months, Seth often came without wearing a shirt. He said, through his talking machine, that he wanted a torso tan. MH always wanted him fully clothed. This issue was a constant summer battle. Seth was also a flirt with all our young leaders and sidewalkers.

The following excerpt was recently written by Seth on his talking machine:

In 1991, I was hit by a car and sustained a traumatic brain injury and was in a coma for about eight months. Because of this I use a wheelchair to get around and a communication device to "speak." I have spasticity throughout my body as well as balance and visual challenges.

I had weekly therapeutic horseback riding sessions at Greenlock for about twelve years. Being in a wheelchair, I'd get into the barn, be wheeled up the ramp, mount the horse with the help of my therapist and away I'd go. Sometimes I rode around the barn, sometimes in the outside corral, sometimes down the hill when the horseflies weren't vicious. Balancing without holding on was challenging enough. Add the sway of the horse or if it should stumble, and you could see why sidewalkers were essential.

I remember demonstrating my riding abilities at equestrian seminars to show the benefits of therapeutic riding to other physical therapists. I also demonstrated riding and answered questions about my communication device to a class of children from the Gordon School.

There was also a newspaper article about Greenlock that had pictures and information about me, and I was also featured in a Channel 6 television segment, called "Horses of Hope" (by Dan Jaenig).

I really think those riding sessions helped my balance and posture. I also like the camaraderie, the sense of accomplishment and the fresh air.

Kevin had Down syndrome and lived in Rehoboth and became one of our riding joys. He was with us for about twelve years and always had a smile on his face. He became known as our official greeter; he greeted and talked with everyone he saw when he came for his lessons. Kevin often rode a horse while engaging in being a fantasy character of a recent TV show he had watched, like *Caillou,* or *Sponge Bob.*

One day after he rode, he saw that Diana, our volunteer coordinator at the time, was trying to find her basset hound, Katie, who had gotten loose. Unbeknownst to all of us, Kevin found Katie behind a shed and reappeared with the basset hound in tow, but he had taken on the persona of Superman, complete with taking off his outer shirt to expose his Superman tee shirt. At age twenty-one, Kevin got a job at McDonald's cleaning lots and lobbies, so he decided it was time to graduate from riding. Since Sheila and I both loved an occasional lunch at this establishment, we would go get lunch while he was there. The greeting we got when he saw us was worth everything! He introduced us to every employee. His smile became infectious, and he had all the other customers learning about us and Greenlock.

Another four-year-old, Isabelle, came to us because she was mute, and she would not talk to anyone – mom, nor dad, nor us. She rode Rocky, a Freckles look-alike, but without the sway-back. Isabelle would follow directions but not talk. One day about six weeks into her riding, she started talking to her horse! For a few weeks, she would talk only to her horse until miraculously she started talking to Sheila. She was a very shy child and Sheila was extremely respectful of her shyness. Within a short time, she became a good little rider and moved on to a regular stable. When she was a teenager, she came back and volunteered with us for about a year.

Over the years, we have seen so many changes in people who have received our services. We serve about one hundred fifty unique people per year and the average length of stay is about three years, which would suggest over thirty years we have taught or treated well over 15,000 disabled people, mainly children and some adults. Parent testimonials over the years suggest that their child's balance is better after being on a horse, their walk is more stable, they are calmer, they are more verbal, and they are able to sit up. The list goes on and on.

Their parents, on the other hand, are very unusual group of people who have and are navigating a world most of us don't even begin to understand. I believe that most women who are expecting babies assume their children will fit the norm. Some may learn in utero that there are problems, some at birth, some during their child's early development when they become delayed or perhaps quirky. Motherhood produces amazing bonds between mother and child, and this is often compounded when you have a child with special needs.

My observations suggest that unless there are major medical complications, the early years with a special needs baby are reasonably easy for most parents, but later, when they are struggling to find ways to occupy their child's time and are also dealing with their autonomy and independence needs, their life becomes more complex and challenging. My suspicion is that this particular parenting is not easy, and sustaining a relationship with one's spouse often becomes strained. It is a known fact that the divorce rates are higher for these parents than for a population without special needs children.

Many of our older riders come from single-parent homes, and the mom is typically the caregiver. Many of these moms have literally given their lives over to their children. One example was our client, Alexis, in her mid-twenties, nonverbal, who needed help with activities of daily living, i.e. bathing, eating, and toileting, and her mom did it all. I often talked with her mom while Alexis was riding. She was a well-educated, bright, woman, married to a college professor, but she had not been out, even to dinner with anyone, including her husband, in fifteen years. No movies, no theater, no vacations, she was with Alexis twenty-four/seven. Mom says she did not trust anyone to take care of her daughter. What a tragedy Mom's life had become!

Unfortunately, there are occasional accidents that occur as a result of being on a horse. A horse can suddenly spook, or trip and fall forward, or suddenly shift around, and riders do fall off. On average, we do twenty rides per day, over six days per week. One hundred twenty rides per week, over fifty weeks a year, so then 6,000 rides per year over thirty years equals approximately 180,000 rides. At Greenlock, we have always trained our staff and volunteers in an emergency dismount procedure, which is amazingly successful in preventing falls.

But the procedure requires a side walker, which our kids in hippotherapy always have, but no such person exists in therapeutic riding. Usually, these riders just have a horse supervisor. We have had occasional falls which only result in some black and blue marks, perhaps a day or two of discomfort, and the possibility of fear to get back on a horse. Most of our minor horse accidents have been sporadic, with one major exception. One day Sheila lost three riders off three different horse at three different times during the same day. For the first one, Sheila was leading Jazzy when she spooked in a hippotherapy session with Mary Helene. The second one was when Sheila was leading Beringer, who tripped while walking on a trail and the rider tumbled forward. Later on, that same afternoon, her last rider, who was part of a group, was in the ring riding Rosebud and started saying, "Sheila, Sheila, help!" Sheila looked at him and saw that the saddle, with him on it, was slowly descending towards the ground. She ran over and caught him. At this point, all we could do was laugh. We still are laughing today; no one was hurt, and all the riders returned the next week.

Only three accidents have resulted in injuries requiring medical assistance and all involved broken arms. One of these major accidents occurred soon after we moved to our new farm. I was teaching a therapeutic riding session and Crystal, a student from St. Mary's School, fell off. She was riding a reliable pony called Shah, a small dapple-gray Arab. She was trotting around our outdoor ring when Shah stumbled in a corner, and Crystal tumbled off and broke her arm. It was an obvious compound fracture in her upper left arm. An ambulance was called and she went to Rhode Island Hospital for treatment. She remained in the hospital for a number of days, had surgery, and finally recovered from the injury. About two months later, I got a call from the school and, unbelievably, they were thanking me. Apparently, she was a student who was up for adoption and was often overlooked at the school since she was not a problem student. While she was in the hospital, she became noticed, and one of the staff wanted to include her in her family. She started the process, which finally resulted in a happy adoption for both parties. Sometimes even major accidents lead to good outcomes.

Groups of riders showing their skills

Greenlock was often asked to bring horses and riders to do demonstrations of hippotherapy and or therapeutic riding. Two notable events were: The New England Dressage Association, which, for many years, had their final competition at Fieldstone Farm in Halifax, MA, and always asked us to do a therapeutic riding demonstration. We demonstrated at this event for about six years, and each year we would bring different riders to show off their skills and achievements. Since this is a dressage event, we often brought riders who would do walk and trot, dressage tests. Gore Place, an estate in Waltham, MA, annually hosted demonstrations of elegant, equine disciplines on Sunday afternoons with picnicking on their expansive lawns overlooking the equine activities. Each year, we would bring different riders and demonstrate what we were trying to achieve.

CHAPTER IX

INSTRUCTORS, THERAPISTS, AND HORSE TRAINING

Greenlock could not survive without qualified riding instructors who have the ability to teach people with disabilities who are often quirky and to train, and maintain a happy herd of horses that want to be working for us.

Over the years we have needed two or three certified riding instructors at any given time. They must be licensed in the state of Massachusetts; relatively easy to obtain and licensed by PATH (Professional Association of Horsemanship International), which has become harder and harder to obtain over the years. We started with Lisa, followed by Sheila and me, and as time went on and instructors came and went, each new riding instructor brought with them a new skill set.

Around 1997, we hired an instructor, Betsy, who specialized in vaulting, and for five years we all learned to vault. Vaulting is a bit like circus riding. The horse is walking or trotting in a small circle, while the rider does tricks on the horse's back with the aid of a two-handled surcingle belted around the horse in lieu of a saddle. At this time, we had a horse, called Printer, an Appaloosa, who was a perfect vaulting horse. The instructor controls the horse's gait through their words and tone of voice, as the horse circles them on a long rope; it's called lunging a horse. My step-grandson, Dan, at the time, was about fifteen and he could stand up on Printer's back as he was being lunged at walk, trot, or canter. Really amazing to watch. Unfortunately, Printer had a condition called moon blindness, which is common in his breed. He became blind and went back to his original home to live out his days. At that time, with our disabled riders, we adapted the process by leading the horse with the instructor walking next to the rider assisting them. All these tricks are first tried on a stationary vaulting barrel. Vaulting is done as an adjunct to riding lessons and really helps with confidence, coordination, and balance.

Dan Laskey, age fifteen, standing on Printer's back as he was being lunged at trot by Betsy, our vaulting instructor

Next, we hired an instructor who became fascinated with natural horsemanship and learned the techniques developed by Pat Parrelli.

Natural horsemanship assumes that the human can try to think like a horse and thereby develop better communication with the horse which forms a relationship based on consistency and trust. We had Parelli trainers come to Greenlock and give three-day workshops with our staff, volunteers, and horses. Our instructor, Ginny, loved all these techniques and tried to incorporate them into her lessons. She also wanted to train all our horse leaders to use these techniques. But, the training is quite complex, takes hours to master, and does not lend itself to being made more simplistic. It's all about a relationship with your specific horse, and relationship-building takes time. Natural horsemanship works well when one person relates to one or two horses and can develop a trusting relationship, but it takes time and work, and it is hard to implement when multiple people work with multiple horses.

Liz Baker also brought us Mary Helene Chaplin aka MH, a physical therapist (PT) who is still loosely connected to us today, and she is a board member and faculty at The American Hippotherapy Association (AHA). MH also embraced Natural Horsemanship and also tried incorporating it into our program. MH is a fabulous therapist, who knows every rule and regulation put out by PT licensing boards, AHA, and any other monitoring agency that exists. Now I'm a person who occasionally thinks outside the box for a practical solution to a seemingly minor problem, and if I've heard it once, I heard it multiple times from MH and others, "I am not willing to risk my license on doing that." The "that" might be having a riding instructor see a hippotherapy client so they can still come and ride because their therapist is sick.

One day, in the early '90s, a physical therapist showed up at Greenlock with an infant in her arms and two toddlers at her feet. Laurel wanted a job with us, although she lived an hour away and was recently widowed. My thoughts were: how is this going to work? Widowed woman, living an hour away, with three kids? Miraculously, it did and she became a part-time employee, and our first formal Program

Director. She had a horse at home and took advantage of acquiring every license and certification that was offered. Because of her being widowed, she and her daughter were eligible for survivors' benefits; thus, she could not earn above a certain amount of income, and as I've said before, Greenlock was always lucky.

Among other attributes, Laurel was a devout Christian. Late one afternoon, Laurel had a late last session of the day with a child with autism, and I was the leader of her horse, Blue, a Missouri Foxtrotter. We were on our trail in the eleven-acre field behind the arena when Blue suddenly grew in stature and went on high alert. I felt he was manageable, and we kept walking, but Laurel started singing Christian songs to calm Blue. Laurel had a beautiful voice and it was a calming and poignant moment for all of us. She stayed at Greenlock for about sixteen years. Finally, she made the decision to move on to a new job, with a less physical way of applying her skills. Her children had all turned eighteen, so she could finally be paid what she deserved.
I reacted to her leaving in a very inappropriate way. To this day it is one of my major regrets. I got angry with her about her leaving. I was truly dependent on her being a part of Greenlock, and at some level, I needed her calming presence. She, to this day, has not spoken to me again, and it is probably justly deserved.

Over the years many therapists have worked at Greenlock. Betsy Wagner, a pediatric PT, worked at a children's hospital and joined our ranks working per diem for a number of years. During her tenure with us, she adopted a child from China as had my neighbor. The two adopted children came to this county from the same orphanage two weeks apart and became childhood friends. To keep Betsy at Greenlock, we set up a daycare in our art gallery two days a week that she worked for us. We had three children in attendance: Betsy's daughter Rose, my neighbors' adopted daughter Gia, and Michaela our barn manager's granddaughter, who lived next to the farm.

Betsy was also known for her love of animals: cats, dogs, etc. She was always rescuing them and taking them to her house. One day she showed up with a geriatric pug in a wheelchair who she had adopted because its owner could no long provide care. I asked about the wheelchair and she explained that they came as male or female chairs, but she only had a male chair and the pug, named Sweetie, was a girl. Sweetie seemed amazingly happy racing around Greenlock in her chair, and finally she peed and out came her – it sure looked like a penis? So, I said, "Hey Betsy, does Sweetie have a penis?" And she than sheepishly told me that the pug was a hermaphrodite. Wow! In today's world that would be trendy.

Betsy recently told me a story of one of her more memorable days at Greenlock. She had had a frustrating morning getting her daughter ready to come to Greenlock and was feeling somewhat overwhelmed with parenting. During one of her sessions that afternoon the horse she was using, Sultan, suddenly stopped and would not take another step, regardless of the leader's urging. Ten seconds later the child on the horse had a drop seizure. The seizure was severe enough that an ambulance was called. Betsy never forgot that day, she credits the horse with knowing what was about to happen. Her morning issues took on a new perspective as she realized what the mom of that child was dealing with.

This was not an isolated example of horses sensing seizures. Over the years many of our horses have shown similar behaviors prior to their passengers having seizures. Horses really are remarkable animals in their ability to sense what's happening to the humans on their back. Another example: if a passenger suddenly becomes off balance on the horse's back, the horse will often sidestep to stay under the rider and try to rebalance them on their back.

Sue Fiske, a PT assistant, started with us at Palmer River and is still with us today. Her greatest asset is that she can solve most human back pain with one or two treatments. She is also licensed as a dog physical therapist, and she works on horses as well. The downside is she thinks every dog, horse, and human at Greenlock always need some sort of stretching, massage, or ultrasound. And we probably do.

Sue is also an accomplished rider and helps train and maintain our equine assistants.

Sue is the only therapist I know who is not obsessed with regulations, rules, and progress notes. She is obsessed with making a difference in every client she works with every time she sees them, even if it means that she violates ending their sessions on time. She focuses on progress and talks about the little boy who never talked but whispered full sentences while on the back of a horse ... or the child who never before sat up independently, but achieved that milestone while on a horse ... and the many kids who took their first, often wobbly, steps after being on a horse. Her progress notes are often written days later or forgotten about much to other people's annoyance.

Sue tells the story of a little girl called Grace who had somewhat older parents, who could be labeled as "helicopter" parents. One day Grace was in a session with Sue and a nearby horse had his penis hanging out, as occasionally they do, and Grace asked, "What's that?" Sue, being politically correct, yet honest, answered, "It's what he uses to go to the bathroom." The session continued in silence for a while and then Grace asked, "How does a horse fit in a bathroom and put his hose in the toilet?"

In 1995, a volunteer named Kathy Darowski appeared at the farm at age fifteen and never left. I'm terrible with names, so I apparently called her Kate for the first six months (we had a lot of Kates at the time), and most teenagers come and go. Kathy just went with it and let me call her Kate until I finally recognized my mistake. Kathy lived in Rehoboth and went to the local high school. She convinced them that she should be allowed to do a work-study program at Greenlock, which meant she could be with us every afternoon, on school time, all week long. Kathy was persistent! When she turned eighteen, she pursued her Massachusetts riding instructor license, and then her therapeutic riding instructor license.

Kathy, early on, decided that she was going to remain at Greenlock for the rest of her life. Her goal became making herself indispensable, especially to me. College time arrived, and her goal was to become a PT. Shortly thereafter, this goal changed, and she became an occupational therapy assistant. Now, she could not only be a riding instructor at Greenlock, but she could also be a therapist. Her goal of being indispensable was slowly being realized.

During this time, she acquired a horse named Toby, an Arab. Prior to his purchase, she had a two-week pre-purchase trial, and asked if he could stay at Greenlock. While he was here, I pretty much ignored him, since he was a high-strung, somewhat neurotic, and a typical Arab horse. But something about him nagged at me. He was a lovely mover. I watched Kathy take lessons on him, and I watched her trainer ride and lunge him. It seemed like Toby did not embrace any of these activities. But, when he was near our herd, and in his paddock, he watched what our horses did, and he seemed interested and settled. I had a hunch that, like Jiminy, he might just take to this life.

Kathy took her horse to her trainer's barn for a month, then to her home for a month, and his training struggled. I suggested he return to Greenlock with the proviso that we try to use him, and if he worked out, as I had a hunch he would, he could stay. He stayed for another twenty years and was always the "world's most neurotic Arab," but he became a Greenlock star.

Meanwhile, if Kathy wanted to stay with us at Greenlock, she would need to become a licensed, Occupational Therapist. This meant money and a three-year commitment to a graduate program. Kathy was not sure she needed, or wanted to take this step. Sheila was also not convinced, but a Program Director position required she supervise other licensed therapists and do client evaluations. An aide cannot meet these requirements. I remained adamant that Kathy needed to enter a graduate OTR program and get this next degree. Finally, a plan was worked out in which Greenlock would use its capital fund to pay her tuition, and Kathy would pay the loan back by working off the amounts and by taking a lower incremental salary after graduation for a number of years. Every semester the bills came. Wow! Did I react!

Graduate school was mighty expensive, and I hate spending money, but the results of her getting this required a degree that was well worth the cost.

One of the larger roles of a riding instructor is to train and maintain our horses in being successful working with us, and in keeping our herd fit, happy, and safe. When a new horse comes to Greenlock, they must be trained to stand quietly at a ramp, where clients either walk up, or are wheeled up, so they can more easily mount the horse. The horses have to be able to tolerate riders doing alternative positions on their backs, like turning backward, kneeling, or even standing up. They must be willing to have games played while a rider is on their back, such as throwing a ball into a basket or ringing bells hanging from a tree limb. And they must be able to handle having a leader, a sidewalker, and a therapist surrounding them during sessions.

This life is not for every horse. Horses, like humans, have different personalities. An old farrier (blacksmith) once told me, "It takes at least a month of being with a horse to get to know a horse." Truer words were never spoken to me on this subject. Unfortunately, most of us buy a horse on looks and movement, and most sellers give a buyer about two hours to make this huge decision. Bringing the horse home, you finally start learning their preferences and their quirks, and they start to learn yours. It's a relationship, and it needs work to maintain it. An example of learning about a horse was Redd, a fifteen-year old Morgan. Great horse, great personality, but he had a quirk. He had been used as a show horse, and trained to go into the middle of a ring and stand in a stretched position stock still. We called it "parking." Every opportunity he got, he would walk to the center of our ring, and park. Another example was Freckles. Fabulous horse, in spite of his sway back, loved by all, but if he had to wait between sessions, he pawed great holes in the ground, either tied or stalled. Patience was not his virtue. Then there was Odin, who ate anything including the shavings that we put in his stall for bedding. Blue had llama trauma whenever the next-door llamas visited his paddock fence line. All great Greenlock horses, but we had to manage their quirks.

Our horses also clearly knew us humans as individuals and had preferences. Go stand in the middle of a herd of horses and see who comes to which human. Or call their name from a fence line, and they will often go to people they know and trust. More importantly, try to give a horse fifteen pills prescribed by a vet for some ailment orally, two times a day for two weeks. This tests a relationship. Jiminy, our Arab, and I had a great relationship. I was almost the only person who could medicate him when necessary. We had a kind of medication procedural pact. You may remember from your childhood, that most medicines have a horrible taste. Thinking you can hide the taste of the medicine in a horse's food is often a fantasy. You usually resort to crunching and dissolving the pills in water, adding peanut butter, or molasses, for taste, smell, and sticking power, and putting the mixture in a big syringe. You must then insert the syringe in their mouth, by lifting their head, and holding it up, until you release the medicine in the back of their mouth. The head must then be held up, until they swallow it, otherwise it will be spit out, usually all over you and the ground. A messy procedure but effective. Jiminy knew this procedure well, and he knew when medicine was coming, but he let me give it to him, as long as I did it his way. He had to nod his head up and down pretty violently about twenty times, without being interfered with, until he was ready. When he was ready, he lifted his head up, opened his mouth, and said okay. It's a daunting experience giving a thousand-pound animal medicine, but if you have a relationship based on trust and respect, it can be easily done, and the horse seems to hold no grudge.

 The characteristics of a horse that will work for Greenlock include: first and foremost a settled and easy-going personality (no spooks, no bucks allowed) and who will allow the rider on their back to do pretty much anything. Size is the next characteristic: not too tall, for a therapist must be able to comfortably work with the person on the horse. However, a variety of heights are needed because riders come in all different shapes. Another consideration for a particular horse is width. Some horses, like Haflingers, are stocky and some, like Arabs, are narrow-based. Again, riders have different abilities in stretching their hip and pelvis so different horse widths are necessary. And lastly a horse needs a symmetrical rhythmic walk that will carry the rider in a steady way. Each of the Greenlock horses must fit somewhere into these requirements so at all times some horse in our herd is able to meet the needs of each of our riders.

Finding horses that will happily work for Greenlock is not a simple process. We reject nineteen out of twenty horses, some because of obvious issues like size, age, and movement, and others based on behavioral issues, like being too strong, or constantly being on high alert, or being too sensitive to touch or sudden movement. When we think we've found the right horse and bring it into our program, our instructors have the responsibility to get to know the horse and to work with him to get him ready for our riders. Occasionally, we get lucky, and a horse comes practically fully trained, and ready to use. Pumpkin, an eleven-year-old Haflinger mare, was an example of this. Within a week she was being used for both hippotherapy and therapeutic riding. She continued for another eighteen years, and everyone loved her. Odin came to us at a very young age, so he needed lots of consistent work and training before he became one of our most perfect horses.

One of the more interesting jobs instructors occasionally have is taking our riders to demonstrations, gymkhanas, and local horseshows. During our early years, when we did more therapeutic riding, we would do outside adventures like this about twice a year. Once we took six riders and two horses – Beringer a big Appaloosa, and Freckles, the sway back pony – to a local gymkhana. Sheila, Pat, and I went as support staff. A gymkhana is a sort of horse show, in which you compete on horseback, while playing some sort of game, like steering your horse in and out of bending poles. It's usually an event based on points for time and accuracy, with only one rider being in the ring at a time. Our riders were entered into multiple walk-trot events, and an instructor could be next to them during their ride but not hold onto the horse. Wow! What a day! Our riders, did exceptionally well, and had a blast. This was what the concept of allowing our riders to be as normal as possible was all about. That's normalization. Greenlock's philosophy has always been if one of our riders could independently walk and trot on a horse, they are ready to start riding at a regular stable. After all, people with disabilities are just people, and wherever possible, they should be part of the community.

∞

CHAPTER X

VOLUNTEERS

Greenlock is a very volunteer dependent organization. Volunteers are used to lead our horses, assist our therapists with walking next to riders, and give general assistance to both running and managing the farm and organization as needed. What a wonderful group of people they are! Some volunteers have stayed with us for twenty or twenty-five years; others make a commitment for a year or two. They come in all ages, although they have to be fourteen years of age to start volunteering. I would guess that we have had at least one thousand volunteers, over the years, with an average of about forty per week.

When a want-to-be volunteer comes to Greenlock, they spend time watching what we do to see if it is something they really want to do. We determine whether they are interested in becoming a sidewalker or leader. Sidewalkers walk next to the horse and help the therapist with the client. The leader is responsible for the management of the horse during the session. If they still want to proceed, we pair them with an experienced volunteer to learn all of our procedures. Volunteers usually come one or two times a week for two to three hours.

Since starting Greenlock, we have had two marriages of volunteers who met at Greenlock. We have had at least two volunteers who changed their names and gender during their stay with us. We have had at least six successful artists, two published novelists, a psychiatrist, two veterinarians, teachers, and countless interns from high schools, colleges, and graduate schools. Most volunteers are memorable for their love of what we do and for all their different, but interesting, perspectives on life in general. Of course, a few provided extraordinary backgrounds and perspectives.

I believe Diana Alexander holds the longevity record for volunteering at Greenlock. She started in 1990 and stopped around 2018. She had recently moved in across the street from Sheila, and Sheila asked if she wanted to help with our new venture. Diana said she had no horse experience, but Sheila said that was not a concern. Diana was always elegantly dressed and coiffed. Her barn clothes looked like my going-out-to-dinner wardrobe. She was a willing learner and graduated from sidewalker to leader in a few months. Diana loved animals, especially dogs. She actually loved dogs better than she liked children, whom she sometimes called "toads" unless they were polite children, in which case their sins were forgiven. Diana usually had two or three dogs at her side, who came with her to the farm. I think Diana learned to do everything at Greenlock from cleaning stalls to assisting with sick animals. We even taught her to ride, although she only wanted to ride very specific horses whom she intuitively trusted. Diana usually volunteered two to three days a week, and in her later years, she became our volunteer coordinator coming on a daily basis every afternoon.

One of Sheila's and my jobs at Greenlock was cleaning male horses' sheaths. Sheila cleaned while I held the horse. Sheila was more obsessed with this than I, mainly because when male horses let it all hang out, it often has a yellowish crust hanging off it, and when small riders noticed, they either reacted with an, "Ooh!" or, "What's that?" or, "That's disgusting!" We felt it was sort of a "Sex Ed" topic, not really our mission. Sheila was undergoing her first retirement, so we decided Diana was the best choice to replace her as our principal sheath cleaner. The day came for Diana to start her apprenticeship. She appeared dressed in her ironed white shirt, designer shorts, and white sneakers, but she got right to work in learning the ins and outs of the job.

Diana learned to do it all. In one of the early newspaper stories about Greenlock, Diana's picture was in the article, and the caption identified her as "the young riding instructor." From that day on, we all called Diana the young riding instructor. Many times, over the years, people thought Diana and I were sisters, although I was less elegant than she, but we were both tall and thin and wore baseball caps, so we just went with it.

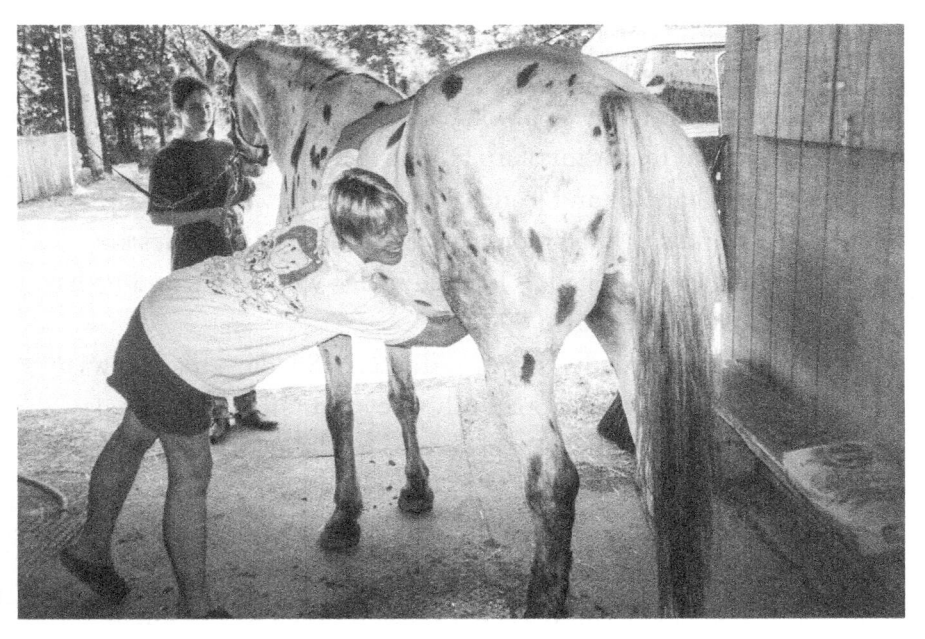

Beringer (horse) with Diana learning to clean horses' sheathes

Ronnie Gomes came to us in 2008. He had been a train engineer and had worked for Amtrak commuter rail out of Boston. He was the locomotive engineer whose train had been hit in Canton, MA, by another, loaded, runaway lumber train car carrying one hundred and twenty tons of cargo. The runaway car had gotten loose from its chalks and started moving down the tracks. When it hit Ronnie's commuter train, it was going forty miles per hour. Ronnie had saved the day by keeping his passengers safe, but he, himself, sustained many major injuries. He lived in Rehoboth, and one of his rehabilitation therapists suggested he come to Greenlock to volunteer to try to get his confidence back as he recovered. He showed up one day, told me his story, and asked if he could help. Coincidently, my nephew, Gregory, was staying at Greenlock, decompressing from a thirteen-month, solo motorcycle trip from here to the Arctic circle, then down to Tierra del Fuego, by going down the east coast of South America, returning up the west coast, and then back here. Gregory was assisting with farm repairs, and Ronnie wanted to try to regain his confidence around working with tools and engines. He and Greg worked together on many small projects. As time passed, Ronnie also became interested in our mission. He started sidewalking and later became a horse handler and leader. Ronnie is still with us doing horse-leading and small farm projects as needed. His injuries are nonetheless present, but he has learned to age with them, and he has been a great asset to the farm.

Lest we forget, Sheila Ryan, yes, a different Sheila. This one was an animal communicator. Apparently, they can talk with animals, even animals they have never met or who have died. I was skeptical, but told Thistle, my golden retriever, in no uncertain terms, not to talk to her, in fact, not to go near her, because I did not want to know Thistle's opinion on any subject. She was the kind of dog who had lots of opinions. Sheila came to Greenlock on the recommendation of Diane Hutton. I had met Diane at the first Parelli National Horsemanship clinic I ever went to. My first impressions of people are often wrong, and in Diane's case, I was convinced she was an upscale, snobby, dressage rider. I was surprised when she said yes to doing the clinic, but it turns out, she was open to try any riding discipline if it helped her and her horse. She had a huge, very young, dapple gray, majestic Quarter Horse. And we had a great four days together at the clinic. She's been a volunteer at Greenlock ever since that clinic. Sheila was a boarder at Diane's barn. Diane thinks the world of Sheila, and she is open to communicating with her animals past and present. I'm a skeptic, but I guess such differences make the world much more interesting.

Sheila was a horse person and so immediately became a horse leader. During her brief time with us, she apparently talked to most of our horses, and Kathy Lizzote, who was another longtime volunteer, recently shared a story with me about how unsettling it was to Sheila when Freckles refused to talk with her. Odin, an ample horse, told her we were not feeding him properly, and we were definitely not feeding him enough, and on and on our other horse complaints went, I guess.

Jane and Arthur Manchester were a brother and sister; both joined us for about three years. For a long time, I could not figure out what they did in life, and they were not quick to divulge their family business ventures. Due to their skills, dress, and vehicles, I assumed it was outdoors and had something to do with animals. They were generous, understanding, and extremely willing to assist with anything. Finally, one day Arthur told me about their business. He prefaced it with, "I hope you understand. We run a slaughterhouse in Tiverton, RI." "That's cool," I responded. It turns out this slaughterhouse caters to different ethnicities who need various animals slaughtered in a particular way due to religious beliefs. Usually, these practices are very humane. So, this started many discussions about animals, their butchering, and their remains. I learned a lot about rendering, hot composting, and the laws around what to do with remains. One day I suggested to Arthur that perhaps he could help us out if one of our horses died. He could, and he did and does. I helped him set up a small venture called "Final Ride," where he advertised with local equine vets about this service he now offers. When he or Jane comes to pick up your animal, they are very understanding and respectful of the situation. Arthur is the one who made me so sensitive to the issues of drugs in horses and how the handling of their remains is different from a horse that dies of natural causes.

Arthur was also the one who caught and took the cow and bull that I had acquired the day I purchased the hay field. He told me they were the only cattle that anyone had ever given him.

Kathleen was a volunteer with us for about two years back in the late nineties. She came two afternoons a week (Tuesdays and Thursdays). She lived in Newport, R.I. She was a Buddhist, an artist, very alternative, and totally committed to our mission. And she became good friends with Pat Rock. Kathleen volunteered at Greenlock before cell phones existed, so landlines were our only source of communication. Kathleen rarely canceled and was an extremely dependable and competent volunteer. One Tuesday, she did not appear, and then again on Thursday, she did not appear. We thought we might have missed that she was perhaps away. Our phone calls went unanswered or went to her answering machine. That weekend, we were having a horse show for our riders and she had signed up to volunteer at the show, so when she again failed to show up we began to get really concerned. She had a boyfriend, a fiancé, who lived in Florida, who called us that same day and said he was driving up to Rhode Island because he was concerned that he could not get in touch with her. Finally, we called the police, who went to her apartment and found her in the bathroom, having aspirated from being sick. What a sadness descended on us and what a lesson learned! This communication omission has haunted me since that day. Pat and I went to her memorial service, which was done in the Buddhist tradition. It was a beautiful, simple, and profound experience.

Pierre, a young man about twenty-one years of age, came to Greenlock in about 2009 and stayed about a year. He was handsome, articulate, competent, polite, and willing to do any job we needed done. Pierre's parents should be proud of this young man. He mainly helped with our sessions, leading and sidewalking, but he also willingly did farm chores when asked. At this time WiFi was becoming more prevalent. The Greenlock house had WiFi, and we wanted to use that system in our office, which is attached to the house. This was a challenge for us, but being young, Pierre was more knowledgeable than we were, so he stepped in and helped. This help included having to acquire additional cables and booster components. Pierre obtained all these necessities, and kept telling us we did not need to reimburse him. It was all taken care of.

Pierre stayed on about another two months and then got a job working at the new local L.L. Bean store in Mansfield, MA. What a loss for us, but we understood. About a month later, one of our physical therapists, Betsy, brought in a newspaper article and asked, "Isn't this the Pierre who has been volunteering with us?" The article was about his being arrested because he was caught stealing L.L. Bean's hi-tech equipment. Apparently, this was not the first time. So sad, but what about all the stuff he had given us? I've never seen Pierre again, but what a memorable and great guy he was when he was with us!

During our early rides, about a year before we started Greenlock, we would trail ride our horses over to Fox Lea Farm on Sunday afternoons and watch them play polo. One of the players, whom we met, was Rob Mariani, another Rehoboth resident. He worked in advertising, authored a memoir, and was a fabulous artist. When he retired, he came to Greenlock as a volunteer and became instrumental in assisting us with our fundraising, especially our silent auctions.

Molly Bliss, a neighbor, and Brown University medical student became involved. She was a world-class rider and rode internationally in many eventing competitions. While with us, she created a program with Hasbro Children's Hospital's rehabilitation department, so they started sending children to ride at Greenlock. Molly decided to pursue her riding license with the then-North American Riding for the Handicapped Association, so she could teach these children. She successfully passed all the hoops with NARHA and then sent her video showing her ability to ride. At that time, they required a video following a specific riding pattern. Molly sent a summary video of her competing at the World Equestrian Games. The video included portions of her dressage, cross country, and stadium jumping, including the international narrative. They almost flunked her because of this violation of protocol. However, saner heads prevailed, because even they realized she could ride. Molly taught these kids for us, a couple of hours a week as a volunteer, until she graduated from Brown, and received her medical degree.

Alicia Hoffman, a distant relative of Sheila's, was about twelve when she started. She owned a horse and had plenty of experience, so we allowed this age violation. When she became fourteen, she asked if she could have her Bat Mitzvah at Greenlock and bring her horse. Of course, she could and she did. Alicia stayed with us off and on until she got her occupational therapy degree. She is about to get married to her long-term partner, and their gift will be a piece of Rob Mariani's artwork.

Ann Louise had just graduated from Washington University as a lawyer. She was in the same law class as my nephew, Gregory, who had told her about Greenlock. Soon after graduation, she called me and asked if she could come out and visit for a week. She had been an accomplished saddle seat rider (a style of riding) in Kentucky where she had grown up. She came and stayed in a local motel, and quickly made herself an indestructible volunteer. In some ways, I think she was in love with my nephew, although my nephew was too much of an adventurer and traveler to get connected to anyone.

Ann Louise came at least three times that first summer, always rented a car, and stayed in a local motel. As a young teen, she had a major accident while driving a pony cart, which resulted in lots of injuries and surgeries. Plates and screws were holding parts of her together, and at this time she was unable to work due to the "toxicity" in her body as an allergic reaction to these metallic substances. Her way of dealing with this was eating a special diet, lots of meditation, endless healing supplements, and occasional acupuncture. (Years later, she returned to the medical profession, had the hardware removed, and was finally healed.) The upside of this was she could spend weeks at a time here helping out. All she needed in exchange was a place to live. So other volunteers stepped up to the plate to provide for her. Kathy Kahn had an apartment so she spent a month there. Kathy Lizotte's sister had a basement apartment, so on another occasion, she stayed there. Her visits were always about a month long and every three or four months she would ask to come back. This went on for two or three years. At that time, we had a Morgan horse called Redd. He had been a champion saddle seat horse, but none of us really understood how to cue him, since we were not saddle seat riders. Ann Louise did; they were simpatico. Once Ann Louise showed us what to do and how to get Redd to do it, all worked well. It turns out, like dogs, it is hard to teach old horses new tricks, but it's possible to teach old people new tricks to adapt to an older horse's ways.

Lest we forget Kris Carter, who volunteered for at least ten years and had unlimited freedom in life, so she sometimes showed up almost every day to help. She was amazingly social with everyone and was always upbeat with a huge infectious smile that made people feel included and relaxed. Over time, Kris learned to lead every horse and always did a reasonably competent job of it. One day, when she asked Sheila and me to include her on one of our trail rides, we said sure. We arranged a time and the three of us went off together. It was only after we had been riding about a mile or so, done some occasional slow trotting, that Kris said "This is sort of fun! It's the first time I have ever been on a horse." We were stunned! The instructor in Sheila immediately appeared and helped Kris through the venture.

Volunteering comes in many forms. Greenlock was given a spectacular stained-glass window of our logo, made by Karen White in 2007. It is a twenty-four by eighteen-inch stained-glass window, and it resides in our art gallery over the front door. Karen was an aide, and live-in nanny, for Leah, one of our very disabled riders, for two years. She often helped by being my sidewalker with this child. The gift was given in gratitude for what we do here.

The Greenlock Board of Directors over the years has been made up of people who also volunteer their time to fundraise and provide oversight to the whole organization. Most who serve on this board stay anywhere from three to six years. An exception to this is our fabulous lawyer, David Gay, who has served for thirty years, kept us scrupulously honest, and has attended to any and all legal questions raised over the years. Additionally, he has an amazing ability to find people who will help us out locating material or money for projects. An example occurred when we need new footing surface material, for our riding arena. David had a local contractor friend donate and deliver three hundred yards of Fibar a material used on playgrounds. Then our neighbor, Keith Mello, along with Joe, Mike, one of our parents, and Tom Nerney, our contractor, spent a day moving out the old footing and putting in the new footing. A huge project all done without cost, by wonderful friends and neighbors.

Arlene Violet was a board member for three years around 2000. Her policy on joining boards was that she would give each board three years of service, support them fully in any way she could, and then move on to help another group. She had great name recognition, from having gone from being a nun, then to law school, and on to become the RI Attorney General, and finally a radio talk show host. We love her and she fully embraced our mission and helped our capital fund enormously.

Kathy Lerner started out as a volunteer who led horses and sidewalked; she later became a board member and took on the role of organizing all our cocktail parties and plated dinners. Even today if we ask for her help, she becomes fully involved with helping us organize the event.

Sheila had two friends: Medhi and Rosemary Khosrovani. At different times, they both served on our board and were instrumental in helping us find constant support. Mehdi runs an architectural firm that designs medical facilities throughout the world. He is probably the best dressed man I have ever met. He would come to the farm for board meetings and events always meticulously dressed. One of our fundraisers was a hoedown at the farm, and we had rented a mechanical bull. Medhi, came dressed in full Western regalia, including an ironed bright red Western shirt with a black vest and Western bow tie. He rode the bull like a pro! Later, we found out, that in his youth he had played polo in Iran.

Scott Martin is also a board member, and his family are neighbors of Greenlock and they have been instrumental in assisting us. They have given of their time and knowledge to build a footbridge over our brook, and a bridge that supported car traffic over a ditch to assist us with parking multiple cars at all the big events that take place at the farm.

Dogs are not to be forgotten, as they, too, have volunteer responsibilities. Over the years golden retrievers have been the Greenlock parking lot greeters. Most kids hug them, some play fetch with them, and others just pat them. If kids come and are fearful of dogs, the goldens can get most kids over these fears. When kids resisted wearing helmets and belts, we would first put them on Spencer, a large very blockheaded male golden. This inevitably made the kids laugh, and become willing to try them for themselves. Tabouli led every horse in the barn. At the end of the day, when we were leading horses down to the barn, she would take the lead rope from the leader and march the horse down to the barn. Unfortunately, she did not have opposable thumbs, so could not open gates and unclip lead lines! At least two other goldens shared this skill.

Recently we asked a group of volunteers what made them like volunteering at Greenlock. The overwhelming answer was they like Greenlock's mission, that they liked being outside in all kinds of weather, and they love working with, and being around animals. Additionally, they love the staff, clients, and other volunteers who come here, and the joy and laughter we all share in what we do. Greenlock would not exist if it were not for this wonderful and giving group of people. We thank you all.

Tabouli leading the horses over the years back to their barn

CHAPTER XI

THE COVID YEARS

March 2020, Covid came to Greenlock as it did to every other business in this country. We were forced to close outdoors for three months to see how the virus progressed.

The media presented this virus in a way that made you think it was going to kill most of us, me included. Initially, no one even seemed to know how it was spread, so the outcome looked ominous. Oddly, I was most concerned about what would happen to my golden retriever Tabouli, and who would look after her after I had passed over the rainbow bridge from this infection. There was little question in my mind because of my age, that I was a perfect candidate to get Covid and be placed on a ventilator if one was even available. At least twice a day for months I thought I had Covid, I dreamed I had Covid, and the media suggested even my dogs could get Covid, so for a short while I would not let anyone even touch my dogs. The rumors of how Covid spread were rampant. Some said it was spread by touch and lasted longest on cardboard, on newsprint, on metallic surfaces, on your mail, or on your groceries. Anything you touched might give you the dreaded virus, along with anyone you talked to, because it might also be spread by people breathing, talking, or singing in your space.

The farm became my safe place from Covid and was my salvation from boredom. The farm was outdoors, no one was about unless invited, and the closing came in the early spring, so it became easier and easier to stay outdoors.

I really believed our horses would like the retirement that we humans had imposed on them one March day, but as time progressed it seemed that they, too, were becoming bored. Bruce Graham was still attentive to our Greenlock horse training needs and he gave riding lessons to Caroline Husher, one of our long-term volunteers, who had progressed on to become one of our licensed instructors, and Kathy Lizotte, another very long-term volunteer. When Covid shut us down, Bruce took it as an opportunity to retire and never be seen again. Caroline and Kathy continued riding and our horses seemed to enjoy their workouts. Other volunteers came and brushed horses, some came and bathed them on warm spring days, or just sat and shared carrots with them. Kathy Darowski came and entertained Toby on a regular basis, Otherwise, she spent the time painting the interior of her house. Joe still took care of the farm and animals, and Courtney, my administrative assistant, worked from home. Our Board of Directors still met using Zoom.

We got the requisite government loan, later forgiven, to keep everyone employed. Finally, in late June we reopened, starting with four clients a day, two days a week. Slowly (it took about a year), we increased to almost pre-Covid capacity. The rules of receiving our service dramatically changed. We took and recorded temperatures, everyone was hand sanitized pre- and post-rides, and alcohol spritzing was introduced to anything that had been touched reins, helmets, or toys by the client. We allowed no siblings to play on the playground, and no family members were allowed out of their cars while we treated their children. We embraced the six-foot social distancing rules and everyone was masked, and/or had face shields. Even though it was summer and we were outside, Greenlock had become militant! By now the world was beginning to understand that transmission of this virus was through breathing, but the restrictions on passing the virus by touch had not fully caught on. With all these rules I wondered how the world would procreate, since fifteen years before we had introduced safe sex to the world, and now we had imposed social distancing between people.

Greenlock therapists and volunteers embraced all the Covid rules. The rules the state of Massachusetts imposed on doctors' offices and clinics were adopted by Greenlock's therapists and volunteers without any wiggle room. Serving people out of doors made no difference: a rule is a rule, and all were meticulously documented in each client's record. If I even suggested a shortcut, which I was known to do, I was rebuffed with "What if the state comes in and checks on our services?" Not very likely.

Post COVID-19 riding requirements

During these early months, our veterinarian's office even sent out an email saying they didn't want assistance from anyone over sixty-five years of age when they made a farm call. Music to my ears, I thought. Now if Joe called saying a horse wasn't eating dinner and was colicking, it was not my problem, since I'm so old I was apparently no longer needed. That lasted about one horse-crisis, and I was back in the saddle, old or not.

The first summer passed, and for the most part, all was well. The holiday season and the cold months were approaching, and vaccines for healthcare workers were in the pipeline. In spite of my staff's insistence on being part of the medical community, they were not included in the definition of healthcare workers, who were eligible for such a vaccine. My annual Christmas party was moved to an outdoor bonfire event at the farm, which still remains the venue three years later. Thanksgiving had been in my garage with the door open and Christmas Eve was on my deck. My husband and I developed a social pod that included our next-door neighbors the Weingards and our friends the Potters, who lived across the street. We all spent many Saturday nights socializing that year, and we all remain good friends. Kathy Darowski and I made a Covid pact that we would remain Covid-safe so she could help me at home and at Greenlock.

During this time my husband, Al, a child psychiatrist, was slowly failing due to heart issues. Al was twelve years my senior. We had been happily married for forty years, and I was his third and final wife. I called myself his "trophy wife," or I was known as wife C. He had had four children with wife A, a very brief marriage to wife B, and then me, wife C. Because of Al's failing health, we had a fabulous 39th wedding anniversary party on our deck pre-Covid with the Greenbaums, the Hutchinsons, and the Potters. Luckily, we had made this decision since our 40th anniversary would have been truncated due to Covid.

Soon after this party I became Al's full-time caretaker. Failing health during Covid was a challenge, the idea of his needing to see a doctor was terrifying, as was the idea that I might bring the virus into the house was also. Al remained reasonably healthy under my care until January 2021. He had always loved to walk and he had been the family morning dog walker for years. Now he continued to try to walk to the barn daily with assistance from his son, Alfred, or his daughter, Liz. Kathy Darowski also assisted him two or three times a week. He really liked walking with Kathy because he trusted her OT training and liked talking to her about the kids she was treating. He needed all this walking assistance because his balance was becoming compromised, and he was at great risk for falls. Unfortunately, he fell in our kitchen in early February. He kept telling me he was fine. By the following Monday, I realized he was not fine and needed a medical consult. This was done virtually and I asked for some home health assistance. A consult with a PT was prescribed and she came to our home the next day. She did not like what saw and told Al he needed to go to the hospital as soon as possible. An ambulance was called and he was taken to Rhode Island Hospital. He never returned to his beloved home again.

Due to Covid restrictions, I was not allowed to see my husband for six weeks. This was the worst six weeks of my life. When I could see him again it was because he had progressed into hospice in early April for his last five days. My husband's remains now reside at the farm, a place he truly loved and called a "magical place." A tree is planted above his ashes. Two of our golden retrievers, Tabouli and Teeko-Too, helped to dig the hole, along with our neighbor, Scott Martin. Later that spring we had a memorial celebration in his honor at the farm. The eulogy, if it could be called a eulogy, was written by Kathy Lizzote. Aside from Scott Martin, his daughter, and the goldens, Kathy was the only other person in attendance at the tree planting. She was so inspired by the experience that she wrote a remarkably moving description of the burial and suggested at the end that Greenlock now had some "hallowed ground." Perhaps Greenlock does have "hallowed ground." An especially generous lady, Kay, who had volunteered for many years at Greenlock, requested her ashes also be spread at the farm. My wishes are for my ashes to be spread on Greenlock's green pastures, and for all my golden retrievers' ashes to rest here.

Al's memorial tree

TREE OF LIFE – EULOGY
Written by Kathy Lizzote

It wasn't a plan, it just happened that way. I was in that place at that time. Edith was carrying some wooden stakes and some rope.

I said, "Working on a project?"

Edith said, "I'm planting Al's tree."

Al has a tree?

A Beech tree.

I love Beech trees.

A Copper Beech tree.

I love Copper Beech trees!

Edith said, "I'm going to put Al's ashes in the hole. It will be the 'in memoriam,' but it's so weird, his kids can't be here. They told me I should plant the tree as soon as possible and the kids live all over the country and can't come now. I'll have to do this alone. Scott Martin is bringing his backhoe to dig the hole. It's weird I have to do this alone."

I said, "Do you want me to stay?"

No answer.

I said again, "Do you want me to stay?"

No answer ...

I stayed for the burial of Edith's beloved Al.

We waited for Scott Martin to come to dig the hole.

As Scott drove in, Edith asked me to go to her truck to get Al's ashes. They were in a bag, in a locked box, inside another box. They were heavier than I expected. I felt the responsibility of a pallbearer: don't drop the box. I felt a reverence.

Back at the site, Scott Martin's daughter, Rosalie, had come. We all watched her father dig the hole. As the mound of dirt grew, the golden retrievers – Teeko and Tabouli – joined in the digging.

Scott helped Edith open the boxes. With Teeko and Tabouli at her side, Edith poured Al's ashes into the hole. As she poured, Edith said, "I promised to bury you at Greenlock, Sweetie. Ashes to ashes, dust to dust, I plant the Tree of Life. I love you, Sweetie."

I felt the reverence of the moment that a little spot at Greenlock became hallowed ground, the resting place of Edith's beloved, Al Darby.

Scott layered soil and horse manure into the hole to the right height. Rosalie held the tree so Scott could position it in the hole without disturbing the root ball. It was a tender moment.

As I walked away with Edith she said a quiet "Thank you."

I said, "That was the best service I've ever been to."

Edith said, "It was short."

I said, "No Edith, it was beautiful."

∞

CHAPTER XII

FINANCES, FUNDRAISING, AND THE BOARD

Greenlock started with $20,000 in a bank account we set up. Our initial monthly income was $500 from each of the eight boarders we inherited. Our expenses were high, including rent, hay, grain, salaries, and insurance to mention only a few.

While taking lessons, prior to renting the farm, I met Jan Tarlow, a woman completing her degree as a CPA (Certified Public Account). In talking, she learned of our plans to rent Palmer River Riding Club and start Greenlock as a non-profit Therapeutic Riding Center. She wanted to help, so she offered to do all our accounting pro bono as long as we had a bookkeeper. She has stayed with us for thirty years. Again, it felt like we were always falling into situations where amazing people came into our lives to support us.

The concept of being non-profit was that we wanted to make our services affordable to anyone who needed them and raise the monies to support Greenlock through donations. The two most difficult tasks of running Greenlock were finding the right horses and fundraising. To this day this remains true.

Our first fundraiser was a horse show at Palmer River that included both our abled and disabled riders in the same show. What a success it was! We raised $2,000 dollars, which at the time felt like a fortune. While at Palmer River, we did these shows four times a year, and it was such a joy to watch all our students be so integrated with all the other riders, competing on a horse in a ring! During these years, we also started our November annual appeal, which has, in some ways, become our bread and butter of donated income.

Over the years, we have had the philosophy that we would only commit to spending our time with fundraising events that would hopefully make well over $1,000. Usually, we did two to three functions a year in addition to our annual appeal. We started with golf tournaments and moved to family festivals, barbecues with corn-hole tournaments, square dances, hoedowns, complete with mechanical bulls, and art show openings. In our milestone years, we would have formal plated dinners or elegant cocktail parties. More recently, we have moved towards an annual event at the farm that includes everything: a road race, food trucks, an open house, "big bucks" raffle with one hundred tickets costing $100 each, a silent auction, select vendors, and an art show opening.

Memorable fundraising moments must be reflected on. I always felt that Sheila should take the lead on fundraising because she was more sophisticated and social than myself, and she knew everyone in Providence. Sheila's mom, Dotty Nelson, was an incredibly elegant woman. She and her friends and family supported Greenlock from its inception. They came to practically all our events, and the Markoff Foundation, part of Sheila's mom's family, became one of our annual donors. The problem was Sheila hated fundraising and did everything in her power to avoid this role, and I was constantly cajoling her to coordinate our functions. Early on, I discovered that if I started to set up an event, she quickly realized that if she didn't get involved, any hope that the event would be a success would be lost. I was once given a pin that said, "Elegance Eludes Her" and what a true description it is! Sheila, like her mom, can be elegant; I strive to be comfortable.

One of our first and very notable fundraisers was at Greenlock's five-year anniversary. Marjorie Sundlun was riding with us at the time, hence we asked her husband Bruce, the then Rhode Island governor, if he would preside over the event. The event was a plated dinner at the Hillside Country Club and included dancing and the requisite silent auction. About eighty people attended and it was a festive and successful evening with lots of dancing. Apparently, Bruce loved to dance and he spent most of his time on the floor dancing with various women. Two days later, I answered a call at Greenlock and it was the governor's office asking, "Who was the lady in the red dress?" I handed the phone to Sheila to respond since the lady in the red dress was one of Sheila's friends. In retrospect, this might have been a Greenlock "Me Too" moment.

Our fifteen-year anniversary was a plated dinner and a wine tasting at Ledgemont Country Club where Sheila and Bob were members. At the time, Arlene Violet, a Providence talk show host and lawyer, was on our Board of Directors. She helped orchestrate the event and was our live auctioneer for the evening. About one hundred and twenty people attended and we had eight high-end items to be auctioned off.

Arlene was magnificent! No item went for less than $2,000 and items went as high as $8,000. The most notable item was a walk-on role in a movie that was to be produced by the Farrelly brothers. Friends of the board's lawyer bought it and about four years later, the movie *Hall Pass* was released. The family who bought the walk-on role arranged a private showing for Greenlock at a local movie theater.

Preceding our fifteenth-anniversary event, we had been offered an eighty-pound bronze cast statue called *A Jump Ahead*, a beautiful casting done by the renowned artist Lorenzo Ghiglieri. It all started when the then-North American Riding for the Handicapped, advertised in their newsletter a bronze horse sculpture from a gallery in Seattle, Washington, that could be shipped to an agreeing center. The center had a year to auction it off at a fundraiser. Monies generated above $5,000 would belong to the center. All shipping costs were paid by the gallery. Little risk was involved so I decided to pursue this auction item. Ten days later, a huge wooden box arrived with the statue, information about the statue, the agreements, and the return shipping receipts if it didn't sell. The statue was so heavy that we did not take it to the hotel that year and saved it for a more local event. Because I felt we needed another year of trying, I called the gallery and got an extension. Time passed and no sale. Two years later, I again called the gallery to discuss the statue's return. The gallery director answered the phone and said that she was the new owner and did not want to know about the statue, and not to call them again. We kept the statue in our conference room waiting to see what would happen. Years passed and finally, I asked our Board of Directors, what should be done with this beautiful bronze statue, that technically we did not own, and really should be displayed in a bank lobby. Our lawyer had it researched: the artist was deceased, and the gallery no longer existed. Consequently, after fifteen years we finally sold it to a place that could display it properly.

Our twentieth fundraiser was called "Diamonds and Denim" and was a formal plated dinner at the Renaissance Hotel in Providence. The name implied that even I could wear comfortable clothes. We raised close to $45,000 at this event. We had twenty-five wooden birdhouses made and each was given to a local artist to paint as they saw fit and then sold for $250 each. Additionally, we had a great silent auction which included a two-week trip to Costa Rica, to a three-bedroom house, airfare included. The next day, auction items were collected by the buyers, but the American Airlines ticket vouchers were missing. They had been accidentally thrown away at the hotel. Trying to straighten this out with the travel agent who had acquired them took weeks, but it finally worked out.

From the very beginning of our business venture, I had two rules that we have never violated no loans and no credit card debt. If you can't afford it, don't buy it. Additionally, I strongly felt that we needed to establish a capital fund as soon as possible and contribute at least

$10,000 to it annually towards our future growth. This fund is solely to be used on major capital projects. Over the years we have only tapped into this fund twice. Much of this fund's amazing growth can be attributed to the economy and to an occasional unexpected and unsolicited donation.

The first unexpected financial gift came as a check in the mail during our third year of operation and has come every year since then. It was from a South Carolina organization called Youth Friends Associates. The same name appeared on the letter each year and the name meant nothing to any of us. All they wanted in return was to be put on our mailing list and to let them know about any fundraising events we were having. We did this and after fifteen years, a woman showed up at the farm one day and introduced herself, and lo and behold, it was the same name as the woman on the letter! Apparently, she lived locally, had heard about us, wanted to help us, and was one of the individuals who could disperse this money. She has never come to the farm again, but the annual check still comes and we are forever grateful.

Morton Hospital, in Taunton, was a not-for-profit organization that chose to become a for-profit organization. When this happens, the not-for-profit capital fund that exists must be dispersed to other not-for-profits. We were in the right place at the right time and our wonderful lawyer, David Gay, was on our board and the board of Morton Hospital, so Greenlock became the recipient of $120,000. Our capital fund grew.

Another random act of kindness came from a volunteer who wanted to remain anonymous. She approached me one day and said she was going to make a donation in a few weeks that was going to make me "very happy." I thought $5,000 maybe $10,000 would make me very happy. The gift arrived in the form of a letter which I slowly opened and there was a check for $100,000. I started shaking, found Sheila, and showed her the check. Rarely were we both speechless. Another capital fund boost!

One day I answered the Greenlock phone and a gentleman, who did not give his name, asked a few questions about Greenlock and then asked if we needed money. I laughed and said we could always use money. It was a really strange call and I sort of forgot it. Three weeks later, a couple showed up at the farm and wanted to know more about what we did. I gave them a tour and answered their rather probing questions, sometimes in my somewhat irreverent way. The gentleman, Mr. Wattles, asked me how we made our money and at the end of my answer, as an afterthought, I told him about the improbable call from the guy asking me if we needed money. His wife then turned to him and asked, "Was that you, Gurdon, who called?" And he nodded. From that time on a check started arriving annually from the Howard Baines Foundation.

Soon after we moved to our new location, we hired Tom Nerney, a Rehoboth contractor to build the addition onto the house which included a conference room. This room had cathedral ceilings with a sleeping loft at one end. This room was built so we could conduct twice-yearly hippotherapy conferences at the farm. Coincidentally, it became known as the Greenlock Art Gallery. I have always loved art and felt art openings might be a good way of raising some funds and attracting outside people to come and see the farm and the work we were doing here. Our first show was put on by Betsy McDonald and focused on her equine art. It was a huge success and led to many more art openings over the years by local artists. Judith Bertozzi, a Rehoboth resident, and an avid Greenlock supporter, had at least five very successful art openings in our gallery. Over the years other artists both displayed their work and organized many shows. Notable among them are Susan Potter, Valarie Weingard, and Bruce Graham. Often, we had local potters, wood carvers, or quilters bring their work to be displayed in the gallery.

The Art Gallery has met many other needs over the years. It has become a yoga studio at least twice and, as previously mentioned, for a while it housed a small daycare program. It's been a retreat for various agencies and provides the space for us to give volunteer thank-you parties.

Newport International Polo has also been good to us over the past twenty-five years. Every July, they invite Greenlock, and selected other non-profits, to join them at a match. This takes the form of an upscale tailgate event, and for every ticket we sell at a price established by us, we get to keep the proceeds. Usually, we sell about one hundred and fifty tickets a year. This is always a fun summer event.

Sheila had three going-away parties over our thirty years and each was turned into a fundraiser. The first was in 1995 when we gave a Happy Trails party at Segregansett Country Club. She sold her house and moved to Maryland where Bobby had taken a job. Five years later they returned to Providence and Sheila rejoined Greenlock for ten more years until they moved to Florida. We had a second retirement party, but she did not leave for long and returned for the warmer months, rejoining our ranks. Finally, she retired again in 2019 at Greenlock's thirtieth anniversary. The oddity about all this was nobody ever said, "I thought she already retired." They just wrote more retirement checks wishing her well!

This big fundraiser was our thirtieth-year milestone and Sheila's, I think, last retirement party. The event was at a fabulous house owned by friends of Sheila's and was a cocktail party with heavy hors d'oeuvres. About one hundred friends came along with a visit from the then governor, Gina Raimondo, and Dan Jaehnig, a Channel 10 news anchor. Once again, we had six items that were auctioned off in a live auction. Of course, I was expected to say a few words, and I realized that thirty years had passed, that Sheila and I had created something pretty special, and that we had developed an amazing friendship. I started my words with the requisite accolades to staff, volunteers, donors, and of course our horses. Then I turned to the subject of Sheila's and my friendship and here is what I said:

"One day recently, a person with potentially deep pockets came to visit our farm. Sheila who was wooing them, introduced them to me, and she said, "This is my partner, Edith." Dead silence followed as the visitor looked at us both. Sheila immediately recovered and said, "I mean my business partner." Wow! In thirty years, this word had a whole new meaning. But the exchange started me wondering. Thirty years ago, we had married our names, and tonight we were having our thirtieth anniversary. Last March, when I went to visit Sheila at her condo in West Palm Beach, she said to me, "Bobby's away, so I thought you could sleep on his side of the bed." Sheila chimed in, "And she did." The party erupted into laughter.

Sheila and I always had the philosophy that our clients should pay something for our services, in order that they value it, but we wanted the costs to remain affordable so anyone in need of our services could access them. That's at the heart of why we are a non-profit organization. The first twenty-five years of our doing business we had an honor system, and we trusted people to take responsibility for making their payments to us. Additionally, we billed groups that came or anyone who opted to get a monthly bill. Others just left their money in a box on the desk at the arena. Trust was at the heart of this system. Over the years, as the business grew, we needed to have an administrative assistant who could bring us into the electronic generation of bookkeeping, and QuickBooks became our financial organizer.

In 2019, a new and young accountant, Marisa Sodini, joined our Board and became Greenlock's new treasurer and accountant. During this time, Courtney, our administrative assistant, was upgrading our billing systems and accounts receivable and this included accounting for every payment made by every person who rode at Greenlock. Apparently, our honor system had some flaws, and not everyone is honorable. The upside is that ninety percent were honest, and some even paid if they missed a session. However, a handful of riders never paid and thought we provided a free service, while others apparently paid only occasionally and paid what they felt like paying. Our new accountant now requires every penny to be accounted for with no wiggle room. It's hard to imagine how a business can ever have a problem with embezzlement with the amount of accountability demanded, but just recently, a parent asked to meet with me privately because a billing issue had arisen, and they truly believed it pointed to monies falling into unknown pockets. We checked and a billing error had been made due to two clients having the same name, therefore a debit was logged into the wrong account.

This Greenlock adventure has been a wonderful and successful trip. It is coming time for it to evolve with new leadership. We can rest easy that we have left Greenlock a financially secure business, as long as future leaders manage it well. My best advice is to remember to laugh.

Edith and Nate (horse) advertising for a wine tasting fundraiser

CHAPTER XIII

MISSION ACCOMPLISHED

In spite of all our improbable moments, I now want to focus on the success of our mission. Greenlock's goal is to improve the lives of people with disabilities through the use of our partner, the horse. The following stories have been written by families who have been or are presently clients and riders at Greenlock.

Jack's Story

My seven-year-old son, Jack, has a rare genetic form of epilepsy called Dravet Syndrome. This condition is extremely challenging in so many ways. Jack's seizures are difficult to control and to stop. He is very limited in what he can do. He has developmental delays, speech delay and gait issues. He is unable to regulate his body temperature. Jack had his first seizure at six months old and has had hundreds since. During an appointment with Jack's neurologist, Doctor John N. Gaitanis, he suggested we look into hippotherapy as a therapeutic treatment for Jack. Dravet Syndrome has caused Jack problems with his gait, along with low muscle tone, therefore we all concluded this therapy would be most beneficial for him.

Greenlock Therapeutic Riding Center was the first location I called.

They called me right back and I set up a time to meet with Kathy to go over Jack's needs and condition. Upon speaking with Kathy, I learned that she was familiar with Dravet Syndrome, which was very reassuring. I had already checked out the website and saw that Greenlock specializes in physical therapy, occupational therapy, and speech and language pathology. This was exactly what Jack needed and where he should be.

I knew the moment I drove up the driveway at Greenlock that this was the right place for Jack. I remember saying to Jack, "I hope they have room for you." They did. A few weeks later Jack had his first ride on Toby. What a hit! I was admittedly really nervous the first few times Jack rode Toby. Having a child who has seizures means he can drop to the ground in a second without any warning, which could easily result in injuries. It is tremendously stressful to constantly worry about that, but Kathy had a plan in place in the event of a seizure, which put me at ease. As I watched Kathy, the handler, and sidewalker with Jack each week, I knew he was in good hands and safe.

Greenlock is such a wonderful place; it holds a extremely special place in our hearts. Jack is so happy when we arrive at "the ranch," as he calls it. Upon arrival, we are always greeted by the two sweetest dogs, Teeko and Woodruff. We look forward to Tuesday every week and it is Jack's favorite day of the week, for good reason. Seeing Jack this happy means the world to our whole family. Jack has gone through so much in his life and he is limited in what he can do. Watching him ride brings us all so much joy. I have left the ranch with happy tears more times than I can count. Papa (my dad and Jack's grandfather) absolutely loves to come and watch Jack ride! He comes with us every week. We both gather rocks for Jack to throw into the pond – one of his favorite activities. Jack always says hi to the very realistic crane by the pond. If George and Charlotte are swimming around, he says, "Hi ducks!" He always has to finish his session by throwing basketballs into the hoop and completing the farm puzzle, another favorite pastime. If the stars align on a Tuesday, we may just happen to see the porta john get cleaned out by the truck, which is another one of Jack's favorite things to see. And, of course, we can't forget the occasional pile of horse poop! Jack would clean up every pile if he could. Without question, Jack would move into Greenlock if I let him.

The Greenlock staff and volunteers are so amazing. They are all so kind and understanding and work with Jack so well. If he is having a difficult day, they switch things up to accommodate him. They take the time to learn more about Dravet Syndrome and his seizure types and safety. They all speak to him in such a gentle and kind way, which encourages Jack to interact with them. Farmer Joe always waves and says hello to Jack. Jack is mesmerized by the tractors and work gear he uses. He could watch Joe work for hours.

Jack has always loved horses, so I knew Jack would love Toby. We both fell in love with him on the first day! Sweet Toby was so gentle, kind, and loving. He had a special talent of alerting the handler of a possible seizure, which I witnessed when Jack rode him. I was blown away. Another one of Jack's favorite things was feeding Toby blueberry Nutri-Grain bars and walking Toby back down to his "house." The week before Toby passed, Jack asked Kathy to walk Toby to his house. He wanted to get off Toby and finish his session early to do so. Kathy was so kind and let him. I snapped a few pictures of the two of them that day and it was as if they were saying goodbye to each other. A week later, sweet Toby passed away. We were and still are so heartbroken by his passing. We only knew Toby for two wonderful years but his impact on Jack (and me) was incredible. I will forever remember the time they spent together. Jack has now been loving his time riding Barney every Tuesday. Barney is sweet and likes to keep moving!

I also wanted to mention that Jack attended two camps at Greenlock, which were organized by the Epilepsy Foundation of New England. I never thought Jack would be able to attend camp, let alone at his favorite place in the world! In addition to riding Toby and Barney at camp, Jack was able to ride Nate, Poe, and Summer, who are all amazing horses with unique personalities. Being included at a camp was so meaningful to Jack and to me. It was truly a gift to know Jack had a safe environment to experience being at camp. One of his favorite parts of camp was brushing Amigo the donkey! I saw all the hard work everyone put in to pull off the successful camps. Everything was beautifully organized, safe, and fun.

Jack has gained so much both physically and mentally from his sessions at Greenlock. He has significantly increased his muscle tone, especially his core. He is now able to sit up straight for the entire session and even turn to the side and back! He has gained confidence and trust. He responds incredibly well to Kathy. He now will wear his helmet without getting upset, which has helped at home when Jack needs to wear his helmet for outside play.

I will never be able to thank Greenlock and the entire staff and volunteers enough for everything they do for Jack. Thank you to Edith, Kathy, Peggy, Kathy, Liz, Rosalie, Emily, Al, Tori, Ali, and Farmer Joe, just to name a few. You're all the best and work so hard; you all care enormously about all of the kiddos and horses, and we love you.

I know I am supposed to tell you how much Greenlock means to Jack, but it means so very much to me, too. I am at ease when I am there, and just incredibly happy watching Jack. I feel included and that we fit right in. I am surrounded by people who "get it," and who want to know more about Jack to help him succeed. I am so grateful.

— Jack's mom

Emma's Story

Emma contracted Citrobacter bacterial meningitis at birth, and secondary to that, lost a major part of her brain and developed a seizure disorder with hundreds of seizures per day. She became non-verbal due to the brain damage and lost feeling and the ability to use her right side. My sister in Denmark has a disabled child as well, who was going to horseback riding at the time. My sister swore by it, saying how great it was to help with sensory and motor issues and that if I could find a place to take Emma, it would benefit her in so many ways. My husband, a skeptic, thought it sounded right up there with crystals.

In September 2001, we moved and because of that had to switch out Early Intervention provider. Sally Gilbert was the PT assigned to Emma, and she introduced us to Greenlock. Emma started riding at Greenlock Therapeutic Riding Center in December 2001. Edith has asked me many a time, how hippotherapy has benefited our daughter. At home, the PT would place Emma on a therapy ball and bounce her around, but if she had had two hundred seizures, she would be sound asleep and nothing would be able to happen at that point. But, arriving at Greenlock, we would place Emma on the horse, and if she fell asleep, Sally would lay her on the horse, and they would keep walking. The movement of the horse while walking, the heat from the horse, the breathing, were all sensory inputs that Emma's body would experience despite being asleep. Something a therapy ball could not compete with.

When Emma started Greenlock, she had already had ten brain surgeries, and she had such a small head and no neck strength, that only the smallest cloth helmet with foam would fit her (not a typical riding helmet), and the smallest belt could almost fit her twice. When she sat on the horse, it was like watching a ten-pound bag of potatoes, slumped over a weight bearing platform which was placed in front of her on the horse.

Over the next five years, Emma actually learned to walk. She just needed something to hold on to. During this time, it was not uncommon to show up and it would be a new horse. The answer to why was always, "Oh, Edith had been watching and thought that maybe this different horse's gait pattern would be better for Emma." Eventually Emma landed on Nate, and they are growing old together.

After many years working on PT skills, Emma transitioned to Liz Morley, the Speech Therapist at Greenlock. She introduced an iPad mini to Emma and taught Emma that she could have a choice as to where to go on the Greenlock property. I think this was the first time Emma discovered that her opinions matter.

Here we are twenty-two years later and twenty-eight neuro surgeries later, and Emma is twenty-four. Emma sits straight on Nate and is practicing holding the reins with both hands while steering under the strict supervision of Kathy, an OT and the program director at Greenlock. After Emma gets off Nate, she stands next to Nate, while trying to brush him using both her left and her right hand. It is definitely a work in progress, but twenty-two years ago I could only dream that she would get this strong.

Emma always had OT, PT, and Speech as well as hippotherapy built into her IEP during her years in public school. Now that Emma has transitioned out of the public school setting and is considered an adult, and she can no longer go to the therapists she has seen all her life, it has been a struggle to find qualified services. At Greenlock they take a holistic approach. It is not about how old the client is, but about what skills need to be worked on, while on the horse.

A lot of things have changed over the last twenty-two years, but Greenlock has been here as the only consistent place during it all. A huge thank you to Greenlock Therapeutic Riding Center, Edith, and her fantastic staff, horses, and volunteers. Once per week Emma gets to come outside for thirty minutes, no matter the weather, and enjoy nature, while unbeknownst to her, having therapy.

– Jette Meglan, Emma's mom

Michael's Story

Our son Mike was diagnosed with autism spectrum disorder on April 17, 2007. He was non-verbal at the time, and my husband and I were ambushed into an unknown world of special needs services and resources on a diagnosis we knew very little about. We were lined up with agencies that would help us navigate the resources for Mike, and it was my mother who heard about therapeutic horseback riding. When the workers from the CEDAAR center were at my house, I mentioned it to them, and Mike was able to get an appointment for a consultation. On the day of the consultation, Mike would not let anyone come near him with a helmet or a belt. I felt that the whole idea of him horseback riding would be a disaster. He also had just developed an unreasonable fear of dogs after my mother-in-law's chocolate lab puppy had knocked him over. We were dealing with reactions to Mike's diagnosis from different family members at that time. Some reactions were helpful, and some were not. Some family members embraced his diagnosis, and some had a harder time with it.

I decided to bring my mother-in-law for some moral support on Mike's first day on the horse. He was just starting to use some language, and he was able to verbalize to me that he was afraid. He only agreed to look at the horses on that first day. My mother-in-law did not understand what horseback riding was supposed to do for him. I did not understand either. It was just a resource that was available to him, and I was willing to take any resource I could. When we arrived, I took Mike out of the car and brought him into the barn. In my highly anxious voice, I explained to Claire-Marie, who was going to be his therapist, that he was not willing to ride, wear the helmet, or wear the belt. She just motioned him over to her and told me to wait outside. Somehow, the helmet and belt were on, and she was walking him up the ramp, and in one quick motion, as the horse approached Mike, Mike was on the horse. I could not believe what I had witnessed. So, I sat outside at the picnic table with my skeptical mother-in-law, and as he came outside on the horse, he looked directly at me and waved, saying "Hi, Mom!" I cried, because it was the first time he looked at me with excitement about what he was doing, and cared about my reaction. I told my mother-in-law, "I think that is what it is supposed to do." He was just three years old at the time.

Since then, we have driven Mike from our home in West Warwick, RI, to Rehoboth, MA, for his ride. Therapeutic horseback riding became embedded into his routine, and served as some sort of "reset button." With Mike's different therapies, we also ensured he was involved in typical activities like Boy Scouts, and music lessons. He played piano, violin, and trombone, and stayed very involved in Boy Scouts, going on adventures like camping once a month, backpacking through Miles Standish in Plymouth, MA, and kayaking three miles down Wood River in RI, camping along the way. Greenlock's incredible flexibility allowed Mike to have all of these opportunities, and after eleven years in scouting, he achieved the rank of Eagle Scout on March 11, 2022. Just three weeks later, he was accepted into the University of Rhode Island's College of Engineering with the award of the Presidential Scholarship. We have been on an incredible journey with Mike, and Red (Mike's first horse at Greenlock), Pumpkin, Toby, Odin, Stellar, Nate, Rocky, along with Edith, Claire-Marie, Kathy, and Emma have all been right there with us to share in his success.

It is time for Mike to move on to bigger things, and sleep late on a Saturday. He has grown into such an incredible young man, all because of the different supports he has had, especially the horses; they showed him how to connect, how to balance, as well as strengthen his core. They showed him how to socialize, and most importantly, they showed him to *ride*. We look forward to the next chapter that he rides through.

The Packer Family thanks Greenlock Therapeutic Riding Center for being there for Mike, and all of us, every step of the way.

Simon's Story

Our son Simon started weekly sessions at Greenlock when he was in kindergarten. He was diagnosed with cerebral palsy as a baby and had done physical and occupational therapy for several years before he began riding. None of the standard therapy he had done has compared to riding in terms of fun, confidence building, and growth.

I remember wondering if Simon would be nervous or afraid to mount a horse, but he hopped right up on Marty on his first day and his enthusiasm has continued since. Every Wednesday, after school, my husband or I bring him to Greenlock for his session. It's the only standing therapy appointment that he goes into with gusto. He is relaxed while he is riding and can work on strength and skill building while chatting with therapists and volunteers. One of the best things about Greenlock is that everyone there has taken the time chat with and get to know Simon and his interests. His love of animals has sparked a routine of trading animal knowledge with Kathy and Emily, the therapists that work with him regularly, and trying to stump each other with rare animal facts. It is very difficult to stump Simon!

Since he began riding, Simon has also achieved many of the goals he was aiming for through therapy. One of his first goals was to be able to ride a bike, and by the end of his first year of riding, it was no longer difficult for him to push the pedals and steer. He is still aided by training wheels, but he can go fast! The comfort he feels on a horse, and the core strength he has built by riding in all positions, including sideways, backwards and on hands and knees, has brought all kinds of other physical activities into focus. One of his next goals is to be able to swim, and we feel confident that he can achieve that this summer!

The warmth and dedication of the staff and volunteers at Greenlock is unmatched. They almost never cancel due to weather, and Simon has done sessions in rain, snow, and heat, as well as plenty in temperate weather. The grounds are beautiful, and he enjoys riding on the trails that wind around the property and checking for frogs and turtles in the little pond. He gets to make decisions about where he wants to ride, and that has helped build his confidence and adds to the fun.

We are incredibly thankful that we found Greenlock for Simon. It is such a special place, and riding there has been integral to his growth over the past few years. We feel lucky that he gets to go there every week!

– Morgan Wizer, Simon's mom

CHARLIZE'S STORY

Greenlock Therapeutic Riding Center was referred to us by a speech therapist through early intervention for our daughter Charlize. She had been having some issues developing speech and fine motor skills approaching her third birthday. We weren't quite sure what to make of the idea of hippotherapy as we had never heard of it before, but we decided to give it a try. My wife and I both grew up in a city, so seeing the farm for the first time was quite a sight. We still weren't really sure how this form of therapy would help our daughter, but it was definitely a beautiful area to be in. Right away, the owner, staff and volunteers were very friendly and helpful, giving us insight into how the process worked and answering all our questions. They met our daughter, did an initial assessment, and asked what our goals were. They guided us through the initial setup and got us started with the program.

We were very fearful this might not work, as our daughter was extremely clingy to the two of us and had a lot of trouble with transitions. The staff at Greenlock never pushed too much and showed so much patience with her. She definitely had her reservations, but the staff were great about keeping her progressing and trying the process, while making sure not to push too much on her at once. While it was sometimes heartbreaking to see her struggle with the separation and transition from being with us to going on the horse, it was a joy to see those first few times when she was actually doing it on her own.

You could see the progress each week, not just in the things we were looking for to improve upon, but also her ability to transition and adapt. Within a handful of visits, she was eagerly anticipating the visits to the farm and getting more and more excited each week. If we could have seen into a crystal ball that it would go from a struggle for her to separate from us to the sight of her walking away, waving bye to us as she happily ran to see her special pony, we would have started the therapy even sooner. In each session with the occupational therapist, we saw improvements in the areas we were looking for, as well. After some time, we noticed improvements in her fine motor skills, receptive language, focus and ability to follow directions.

While seeing the hippotherapy work was definitely what we were looking for when we signed up, it was the fun for our daughter and the whole family that was a pleasant surprise. Charlize really enjoys her sessions and gets excited about them each week. She gets very happy anytime she sees a horse in another situation and even calls them and all stuffed animals and pictures of horses, "Poe" (the name of the horse she rides). Seeing her smile each week and the pride she shows with each improvement assures us it's been one of the best decisions we made for her.

With such a beautiful property, the rest of the family has been able to enjoy the benefits of being there as well. Charlize has an older brother, Tristan, who accompanied us many times to Greenlock. While he did not do the horse riding, the play area, the beautiful trails and animals on the farm made coming each week his favorite thing to do. In particular, the two golden retrievers, Teeko and Woodruff, became his two favorite things in the world. I have never come across two calmer and more kid-friendly dogs in my life. He could not wait all week to get back and play with those dogs. He would get so excited to see them when we pulled up and they would always come running up to greet him.

Overall, we have nothing but positives to say about the programs, staff, and volunteers at Greenlock. Not only were they helpful in getting our daughter the help we were looking for, but they provided us an activity that she and the whole family have been able to greatly immerse ourselves in and enjoy. It is a beautiful place filled with some of the friendliest and most helpful people you will ever meet. It can be so stressful to place your trust in something like this with your children, but it was such a joy and relief to see the positive effect and happiness it created for our beautiful little girl. We went into this with a very limited idea of what we were getting into and over a year later we can't imagine having never had this be a part of her life and development.

Thank you for giving us the opportunity to write this for Greenlock!

– *Sincerely, Gary & Katie McPhee*

Ryder's Story

My son, Ryder Lefevre, has been attending weekly lessons at Greenlock Therapeutic Riding Center since October 2021, when he was seven years old and in second grade. He has a diagnosis of Down syndrome, ADHD, and a seizure disorder. Edith, Kathy, and the staff that have worked with him over this time have been extremely patient with the unpredictability of his demeanor, with the frequent changes in schedule due to doctor appointments, and the unexpected occurrence of medical emergencies or medication changes. They have all shown compassion for his well-being and tolerance with flexibility within his lessons when he just isn't quite 100% himself.

They all are very personable with him, gentle toned, and willing to vary the lesson styles and tailor them to his moods and abilities at the moment. A perfect example of this was when the horse he was riding got spooked by a neighbor cutting down trees and Ryder came off the horse. Luckily, the three staff members were prepared and attentive and grabbed him off the horse. He fell onto one of them instead of the ground. The handler got control of the horse and walked him through the woods, right after they had Ryder get back on the horse again to continue his lesson in the barn. We were all shaken up after the incident, but were reassured that the best practice is to get back on the horse, even if/when both the rider and horse are scared. My son was very apprehensive for the next few lessons, yet the staff was flexible and mindful to continually talk him through his feelings and to slowly get him from walking the horse to getting back on to complete his lessons on the horse.

These lessons have improved not only his physical strength and endurance, but they have also enhanced his self-esteem and self-confidence to try things that are difficult, scary, new, or uncertain. The lesson time spent on the horse has been a unique experience that couples the horse and games, academics, and gross motor/fine/social skills as well. He is becoming so brave, as well as confident, as he shows off the tricks he is learning and wants me to capture in a photo; like the times he stands on the horse and is a "dare devil." This has truly been a wonderful experience to witness as his mom, as he is thriving and maturing in so many ways, week after week!

From the owner to the staff members, to the volunteers, everyone we have encountered in our time here at Greenlock has been welcoming, personable, informative, and genuine. I am thrilled he has enjoyed this experience wholeheartedly and that he looks forward to putting on his little cowboy boots on "Friday, Greenlock day."

– Much appreciated, Nicole Perry, Ryder's mom

Katie's Story

Katie had a premature and traumatic birth. After an extended stay in the hospital, she was sent on her way, off to begin a "normal" life.

After six months or so it became clear that she was not making her expected milestones. Early Intervention referred her to a neurologist. It was determined that because of her traumatic birth, Katie suffered brain damage resulting in a diagnosis of Spastic Quadriplegic Cerebral Palsy.

She began wearing glasses at nine months old due to visual impairment and got her first wheelchair at age three. Katie has impaired speech, often drools, and has limited use of one arm. She could not sit up or hold her head up without proper seating, belts, and straps.

For many years Katie received physical therapy and occupational therapy at Hasbro Children's Rehab. At around age nine, Hasbro offered Katie a free nine-week trial at Greenlock Therapeutic Riding Center. We lived in Warwick, RI, and Greenlock was in Rehoboth, MA, but it would be short term, so we decided to let Katie try hippotherapy.

Katie would meet her first horse Arthur, her PT, Betsy, and side walker, Al, at her first session. Betsy was kind and reassuring and honestly, I do not think Katie felt fear that first day at all. Al was a grandpa-like figure who enjoyed humming and singing softly as Katie rode. Another comforting and calming thing about Greenlock was that there were always the cutest, sweetest well-behaved dogs hanging around. On this first day, there was an extremely exhausted golden retriever named Spencer sleeping in the doorway near the barn. We would come for more than a year before we would catch Spencer awake. Diana, a volunteer, always came with a carful of dogs. Kathy became a foster of puppies so there were always cute pups around.

Katie was lucky enough to receive a second free nine-week trial from Hasbro and so she stayed on at Greenlock. Over time we learned Al was a medical doctor and Edith's husband. Katie was very receptive to him and enjoyed seeing him every week. Riding Arthur began to reap some rewards. When Katie was trying to have conversations on the horse, she learned that she needed to hold her head steady and stabilize her trunk. It was not overnight, but it was steady progress. To Katie, it was not the chore she found conventional PT to be. It was fun, it was her sport. She looked forward to seeing Arthur, Betsy, and Al. In the early days, she would ride facing front, then ride facing backward. We would learn that this gave a better stretch to the adductor muscles.

After the trial weeks expired, we decided the cost was minimal compared to the reward. My dad, Katie's papa, would slip her five twenties once a month to cover her $25 a week therapy. Back in those days, hippotherapy was not well known and while "normal" PT was covered by Medicaid, hippotherapy was not. Because of Edith and Sheila, hippotherapy became accepted as an accredited method of Physical/Occupational/Speech therapy. After a year or two, Medicaid of Rhode Island recognized hippotherapy as a covered service.

A year or so after Katie started riding, her horse (now Jasmine) startled while in the barn and Katie had to be "airlifted "off. Betsy and Al made sure Katie got off safely. I remember Al took Katie over to the mat and asked her if anything hurt; humming until she calmed down. It was snowing that day, so Al went outside to get some snow to ice Katie's ankle. She was back on the horse the following week. For my part, I was glad to see they had a plan in case of emergency and to hear they practice these in mock emergencies.

Years later, Nate spooked at the far end of the driveway and Edith told us we had to get Katie off. That was fine, except by now she was a teen and tall. I could not carry her back to the barn so Betsy, Edith, and I had to manage to get her back on the horse from ground level. I could not do that now unless there was adrenaline involved.

It is now over twenty years since that first nine-week trial. Katie is still coming to Greenlock weekly. Katie's "posse" changed from year to year (Betsy, Casey, Laurel, Jen, Kathy, and Katie), horse to horse (Arthur, Blue, Coda, Pippin, Odin, Jasmine, and Nate) but there was no mistaking that coming to Greenlock was giving Katie far more than PT. It gave her a community of friends.

Katie knew for sure that every week she would laugh, get caught up on everyone's private lives, share her own news and laugh some more. Edith and Kris, a volunteer, were the funniest. Oh, remember the time Kris had to go cold turkey off the Bravo channel. Or when Edith started singing the national anthem or something like that when Laurel, a gifted singer, was working with Katie. We can still picture Laurel rolling her eyes.

We still crack up about the many times Edith was the leader. She would start the most inappropriate conversations with Katie and get her laughing so hard she could barely sit up. Laurel found the session counterproductive when Edith was assigned to Katie, but those where the sessions Katie loved the most.

There was the time in late spring when Katie's wheelchair got stuck in the mud and we could not move it. It took about six of us, but we got her out of the chair and into the van so that we could lift the chair out of the mud. That parking spot is now taboo for us.

The staff at Greenlock knew of Katie's huge interest in WWE Wrestling and as fate would have it, a Greenlock volunteer Gary turned out to be "Nature Boy" Gary Gold, a wrestler with the UCW. Somehow it was arranged for him to sidewalk with Katie. They talked wrestling and he left her with some of his memorabilia. That was a momentous day for Katie.

Today Katie is a thirty-two-year-old woman, still coming to Greenlock for weekly hippotherapy. She is a success story in terms of her physical achievements since starting at Greenlock but coming here has really given her so much more. It is an intangible that comes with feeling a sense of acceptance, community and friendship and shared experiences.

– Katie and Janet McAuslin

Devon's Story

Devon's first word was horse. Mind you, she didn't say her first word until she was six years old and even now, she only says about five words. Not coincidentally, Devon started riding at Greenlock Therapeutic Riding Center at age six. Devon is now twenty-nine years old and for the past twenty-three years, the most therapeutically effective, joyful and treasured part of every week, of every year, has been riding at Greenlock. We are so grateful beyond words to the extraordinary leadership, staff and volunteers at Greenlock, who give so generously of their time and expertise with dedication, humanism and heartfelt investment in each and every child.

Devon was born with a chromosomal anomaly. It is very rare and as such doesn't have a "syndrome" or simple name associated with it. The diagnosis a genetic description; Isodicentric 15 or Duplication 15q referring to the 15th chromosome that is affected and the culprit of a myriad of symptoms including developmental delays, seizures, mitochondrial dysfunction, trunk and muscular weakness, incontinence, impaired communication, decreased vision, non-verbal, autism spectrum disorder ... the list is long. For us, Devon is just Devon who needs our love and support. We pick and choose one of the above labels when needed that best helps us obtain services she needs. Thankfully, one of those justified services was Hippotherapy and Greenlock Therapeutic Riding Center was the place.

Caring for a special needs child/adult requires a village. That's not just a saying, it's a reality. Marriages may suffer, siblings are affected, and the family calendar can be dominated by doctor appointments, testing, therapy visits – sometimes forgoing other events/opportunities- and "outings" have to be orchestrated with wheelchairs, medications, food, special utensils and cups, undergarments (we no longer call them diapers at a certain age), change of clothes, etc. For us, the one unified and high priority goal was to get Devon to hippotherapy every week. Why? Because she *loves* it! For twenty-three years the one true joy and most effective therapy has been riding at Greenlock. Did I mention her first word was horse (not Mom) and that she is the most vocal (a virtual chatterbox of five words and multiple sounds) when she is on one of the beautiful horses at Greenlock? The co-treatment provided by physical therapy, occupational therapy, speech therapy and the horse also resulted in Devon acquiring her second word: "ball," which was incorporated into her ride and developing the skill of placing a ball in a basket. So, the village made it happen; changing work schedules, schlepping Devon's infant brother in the car seat, Auntie Mimi, Devon's nurse ... all-hands-on-deck to get Devon to her beloved hippotherapy at Greenlock every week. She rides in the heat of summer, rain and snow, and only COVID could (briefly) keep her away.

Devon started riding at Greenlock in 1999 and I have accumulated many photographs that beautifully chronicle her twenty-three years at Greenlock and counting. I still marvel at how small she was sitting high atop Sultan, the first horse she rode, a beautiful and gentle giant. He seemed to sense every shift in her tiny body and keep her safe with his steady gait and graceful sway. In the November/December 2000 issue of *Animals* magazine, Devon was included in an article titled "Hooved Healers" featuring Greenlock Therapeutic Riding Center's beautiful wooded trails and green pastures, the magnificent horses, and the dedicated staff with photos and stories of children benefiting from hippotherapy. As a proud mom, I shamelessly wrote to the editor, obtained several copies of the magazine, and sent them to friends and family. Many years later while visiting family in Rome, Italy, unbeknownst to me, they had beautifully framed the article and it was hanging in their family room. Needless to say, there were many tears shed that day with humble gratitude for Greenlock Therapeutic Riding Center and all it has done for so many as a timeless source of joy and optimizing life.

Over the past twenty-three years, there have been many horses and many therapists and volunteers who have worked with Devon. We remember each one of them well, knowing their names, manes, and faces captured in photographs and preserved in our hearts forever. I have put together albums for Devon and she loves to look at these photographs. I love to look at them as well. I marvel at her growth physically and the way she engages and interacts when she is riding. Devon's muscle tone is low, she slouches a bit and often curls up like a baby in child's pose. And yet, when she is on a horse she's upright, heels down in the stirrups, and her long brown braided hair sneaks out from under her helmet and trails down her back. In the photographs of Devon riding, she often has one hand waving in the air with excitement, making eye contact and babbling contentedly with the Greenlock team that surrounds her; the horse leader, therapist to her left, and sidewalker to her right. There are photos of horse shows at Greenlock and the ribbons she won that are still on Devon's bookshelf, along with themed events in the barn, and of polo in Newport to raise money for Greenlock. There are photos of Devon and her brother Zachary who accompanied her to Greenlock countless times over the years. And photos of Devon's devoted Auntie Mimi (who loves to take her riding) making baskets for fundraising, and chatting with Edith, the matriarch and heart of Greenlock who makes it all possible.

The photos tell the story of a special child and the magic of Greenlock. A place where essential and effective therapy is given in the setting of acceptance, safety, and love, and accomplishments no matter how small are celebrated in big ways. Greenlock's staff and volunteers are skilled and dedicated, the horses are patient and powerful hooved healers, the children are treasured, and families comforted. Over the years the horses change, the seasons change, the staff and volunteers vary, but the excellence of Greenlock is ever present. Truly, one of the greatest gifts in Devon's life is Greenlock. It is her joy and passion. Words cannot convey the enormous gratitude we feel for Greenlock and the extraordinary team of horses, staff and volunteers that make such a difference in so many lives.

– Vicki Miller, Devon's mom

Piper's Story

Piper loves Thursdays! It's our special day together – Grandma and Piper!

We do the same thing every week … I pick her up from school, give her a special snack, and we hop into the car to go to hippotherapy at Greenlock Therapeutic Riding Center.

Piper has a few very rare genetic syndromes along with hearing loss, low muscle tone, weak core muscles, and balance challenges. Greenlock has made such a difference for her! It is Piper's happy place and she looks forward to it every week. Mr. Al, Maggie, and the amazing staff and volunteers have been incredible with her – they just "get it." Piper works on building her core strength, self-confidence, speech, socialization, and so many other skills through OT, PT, and speech therapy while having fun on her horse. Piper has no idea how hard she is working because she is having so much fun. I love watching Piper's confidence blossom as they take off, Piper on her horse, Stellar, sitting tall and forward, surrounded by at least three adults to support her when needed and returning to the barn, sitting backward with a huge smile, and loving every minute!

An added plus with Thursdays is that Greenlock happened to pair Piper up with another little girl, Chloe. Chloe and Piper have been riding together on Thursdays for two years now. Chloe and Piper have developed their own friendship and look forward to riding together, and doing exercises together while on their horses, such as playing catch with a ball and working on social skills. They work on the girls' balance by having them stand on the horses' backs and wave. They will kneel on the horse and ride sitting sideways – always surrounded by the adults. When they are finished with their lesson, the girls will often have a little playtime at the play area at Greenlock.

Chloe and Piper have found strength in their budding friendship, learning the gives and takes of relationships. They are learning to respect each other, share their ideas and become good listeners to each other and most important, good friends close in age with some similar challenges.

An unexpected bonus for me besides spending precious time with my sweet little Piper every Thursday is getting to know Chloe's grandmother, Priscilla. We have so much in common and really enjoy our time together too. We have many similar interests and like to share our stories and thoughts. While the girls ride, Priscilla and I have gotten to know each other and become friendly too. We sometimes go on a long walk together while the girls trail ride or we will just hang out in the barn chatting the whole time. We text often and keep each updated on things with the girls, ourselves, or just to say hi.

Greenlock Therapeutic Riding Center has been a godsend for us! The attention that is given to Piper to help build her core, strength and self-esteem, and overall confidence is amazing! Add in the new friendships growing between the girls and grandmothers is awesome! It really does take a village, and we are so lucky to have Greenlock in our village!

Wolf's Story

My first grandchild, Wolf Windham Terry, had just been born in Brooklyn, New York. It wasn't long before we realized that too many milestones were being missed. After extensive testing, diagnostic MRIs, ultrasounds, and some surgeries, all of which were soul-wrenching, he was diagnosed with bilateral polymicrogyria, an extremely rare neurological disorder for which there is no known cause or cure. Though he cannot talk or walk independently at this time, Wolf is a beautiful and happy child of seven. He is extremely expressive and loves to hug people.

Having learned about hippotherapy, we signed Wolf up for Greenlock as my daughter and her family had relocated to Rhode Island. When the call came saying that they were ready to do the intake interview, I accompanied my daughter and Wolf. Any concerns we had were assuaged by Kathy Dabrowski's manner of acceptance and easy laugh. She remained unfazed by Wolf's silence, and best of all, she and Wolf seemed to bond almost immediately. He, Kathy, and the Haflinger, Pumpkin, started working together the next week, and what a happy group they were!

As we approached the "Art Gallery," we noticed a sign that said, "Volunteers Needed." My daughter's quick glance at me confirmed that she knew what I was thinking: I have loved horses my entire life, started riding as a child, and most of my life was spent with children of all ages and abilities. I retired from many decades of teaching just before Wolf was born, and this opportunity might be perfect for me. I signed up on the spot. Kathy accepted me as a volunteer right away. I began as a sidewalker and quickly moved on to be a horse leader. Being a part, even a small part, of a child's growth is an extraordinary experience. I have learned an enormous amount about the world of children with special needs and their families, and it has been a great joy to have witnessed many children growing with huge strides or even small steps forward, thanks to hippotherapy. And in a wonderful way, my volunteering has been not only fun and rewarding but also somewhat cathartic as our family deals with Wolf's challenging condition.

One of the most appealing things about Greenlock, after the children and the horses, of course, is the community of therapists and volunteers. Not only is it a beautiful place, but it is also a hopeful and cheerful place, not the slightest bit depressing or sad. Everyone is there for the children and everyone is friendly and helpful. When there is a need, someone, often a volunteer, will fulfill it. My whole family enjoys Greenlock, from the fall festivals to the polo matches, to the art shows in which we participate.

The tenor of an educational community is set by the principal(s). A successful school with a happy faculty, staff, and student body almost always has a terrific leader. With Greenlock, Edith and Sheila are the leaders who have created this truly amazing place. My family and I cannot thank the staff and volunteers, and all the other awesome people who have worked with Wolf and so many other special needs children, enough. I look forward to spending many more incredible years volunteering at Greenlock. We are hoping to see Wolf walk this year, and when he does, we will be celebrating at Greenlock!

When Edith approached me to work with her on this book, I was intrigued. She admitted right away that she is dyslexic and needed help with editing and other aspects of writing. She laughed, commenting that her English teachers would never believe she could write a book, but she has and I love it! Congratulations, Edith!

∞

CHAPTER XIV

EPILOGUE

(This epilogue is a must-read, for it includes a non-traditional approach to acknowledgments; and I have been told never to start a sentence, let alone a chapter, with this overused, overlooked word "so.")

So, I'm a person who thinks outside the box and I'm also a person who reads a lot. My experience suggests that your average reader never reads the section labeled "Acknowledgments." Perhaps the only people who read this section are people who are acknowledged or people who feel they should have been acknowledged. My intent is to invite my readers to read and embrace this section, and think of it as an epilogue about acknowledgments.

I will acknowledge a very short list of people, not because the list isn't long, but because an overlooked person is a person who will remain upset by omission. I am uneasy with people who are upset.

One big thank you must go to Carolyn Windham, my editor, and, it turns out the only teacher who finally managed to teach me how to use the correct tense, use correct grammar, and punctuation. During my early education, I struggled with academics, most specifically reading, writing, and spelling, although I did learn to diagram sentences, but to this day I have no idea why I needed this skill. While writing this book, and working with Carolyn, I finally grasped the concept of tenses, grammar, and punctuation, and my spelling deficiencies were corrected by autocorrect and Siri. Once again, I discovered I learned by doing, not by being told how to do something. And Carolyn was masterful at shaping my ability to write and successfully incorporate the tools of grammar into my text. Thank you, Carolyn, for finally teaching me what other teachers had failed.

Thanks, also, to my numerous draft readers. You know who you are. Every one of you made this a better book. I had eight female draft readers, three male draft readers, and two readers were under the age of twenty-five. All the female draft readers were overwhelmingly worried about tense, grammar, punctuation and story flow with only occasional thoughts on structure. My male readers seemed more focused on giving feedback on organization, structure and content with less worries about punctuation and grammar. Interestingly, my two young readers totally ignored grammar and punctuation, and their focus was: Is it a good story? In retrospect, I wonder if the women, who all knew me, were less likely to want to upset me and so focused on stuff that was more inconsequential to my feelings. The men, who also knew me, were less worried about this dimension so could talk more easily about organization, structure and content. Whatever, every draft readers' thoughts and suggestions were all valued and many of them were incorporated into the final product.

Alisa Forney brought technology to the process. Every edit, large and small, was sent to her to be incorporated into the final formatted Word document, including film and digital photos. Our logo was incorporated into the watermark on each page of each draft. Thank you for being young and being able to make this leap happen for me.

Greenlock staff and volunteers, past and present, should be thanked for being part of my memory, and for allowing me to interview them about their memories versus mine. Memories are a tricky business, especially as they age. Sometimes our versions of the same event were different but with solid reflection, I could often straighten out the tangle of our memories, while at other times they remained just less tangled. Almost every person I mention in the book has read their story and many stories were edited around their concerns, memories, and reflections.

Lastly, parents, and what a helpful group they were! They were given free rein to be honest about Greenlock in all its aspects – good and bad. And except for, of course, punctuation, tense, and spelling, their thoughts were unedited. If a small edit did occur, it was read by them and approved before becoming part of the story.

The mystery of what to do with the book once it was essentially finished had to be addressed. I knew this was not a *New York Times* best seller, and I figured my target group was pretty niche: mainly women, perhaps parents of children with issues, or people who liked animals, maybe people in the field of therapeutic riding, although they might frown on my approach, and, of course, my friends were a captive audience who had little choice. I know nothing about publishing, and I did not have a clue where to start, but based on various scraps of advice I decided self-publishing was the way to go, and of course Amazon was the leading choice among the options.

Susan Potter, an artist, a friend, and an emeritus Director of our Board, created the whimsical artwork map of the farm found in the chapter called 'The Move." I love it and thanks. You're a great artist.

I was told soon after completing the book that now I needed a cover. Paul Weingard, a board member came to my rescue. He made it clear to me that the book cover is the first line of advertising in selling your book. Counter to all I've heard, books *are* judged by their cover. Paul, and his artist wife Val, created a fabulously inviting cover that will certainly engage readers to investigate this book. Thank you.

And lastly I want to thank Randy Walters. He got the book published! And I just handed him the various pieces needed, text, pictures, and artwork, and *voilà* – a book that you could touch, open, and read. What a fabulous adventure this has been! No one I have ever known would have ever predicted that I would accomplish this feat, but all the support I have gotten made it a reality. Thank you all. You're great, loyal and supportive friends.

GREENLOCK

Made in United States
North Haven, CT
28 January 2024